GOD'S PLAN UNFOLDING

STRENGTH AND RENEWAL IN TIMES OF CRISIS

www.GodsPlanUnfolding.com

Glen Aubrey

Creative Team Publishing
Fort Worth, Texas

Disclaimers:

- Due diligence has been exercised to obtain written permission for use of references, quotes, or imagery where required. Any additional quotes, references, or imagery may be subject to the Fair Use Doctrine. Where additional references, quotes, or imagery may require source credit, upon written certification that such a claim is accurate, credit for use will be noted on this website: **www.GodsPlanUnfolding.com.**
- The opinions and conclusions expressed herein are solely those of the author and/or the individuals and entities represented. This book is unashamedly a book of religious faith in God, and reliance upon Him as Sovereign Lord, in or out of crisis.
- Views and opinions are quoted with permission, and are presented without regard to political affiliation(s). Opinions and conclusions of Contributors are limited to their telling of the facts, experiences, and circumstances involved.
- No professional, psychological, or medical advice is implied, stated, or offered in any way whatsoever. You are encouraged to seek professional help, education, advice, and counsel from individuals you deem competent should you desire to learn more about these topics and

circumstances: the reality and effects of the 2020 COVID-19 Pandemic, economic crises from business closures, church closures and/or restrictions, quarantines, controversies and debates over policies and procedures, mixed reviews regarding the efficacy of facial coverings (masks), the effects if any on children and schooling, age-sensitive concerns including but not limited to people deemed "high risk" regardless of the reason; multiple news media reports including accuracies, inaccuracies, and bias whether proven or presumed; protests, violence including but not limited to civil unrest, riots, burning of cities and destruction of personal and professional property, crime, political implications relating to national, state, and local elections if applicable; the topics of racism, Christian spirituality, and Godly responses of faith, renewal, and endurance; God's timing and supreme authority over His creation; human behaviors apart from, or as parts of learning, following, and obeying Scripture; confidence in God's timing, topics of worry, fear, and losses of all kinds, including death and illness regardless of cause, resulting grief, stresses on families, or additional related topics.

- Note: certain names and related circumstances may have been changed to protect confidentiality. All stories where names are mentioned are used with the permission of the parties involved, if applicable. Any resemblance to past or current people, places, circumstances, or events is purely coincidental.

Scripture:

- All Scripture references are quoted from the New International Version (NIV) of the Holy Bible, unless otherwise noted. **New International Version (NIV) Copyright © 1973, 1978, 1984, 2011 by Biblica**

WEBSITE DESIGN: RANDY BECK WWW.MYDOMAINTOOLS.COM
COVER DESIGN: JUSTIN AUBREY

ISBN: 9781735018928

PUBLISHED BY CREATIVE TEAM PUBLISHING
www.CreativeTeamPublishing.com
Ft. Worth, Texas
Printed in the United States of America

God's Plan Unfolding

Strength and Renewal in Times of Crisis

Glen Aubrey

"Stop telling God how big your storm is and start telling your storm how big God is."

~ Pastors Nate and Amanda Grella
Compass Christian Church, North Fort Worth, Texas

Note: This quote was used by Pastor Nate Grella in a sermon in September, 2020. I learned following this sermon that this quote was often used by Amanda's grandmother.
Original author unknown.

Selected Scripture

*****

2 Thessalonians 2:16, 17

16 May our Lord Jesus Christ himself and God our Father,
who loved us and by his grace gave us eternal
encouragement and good hope, 17 encourage your hearts and
strengthen you in every good deed and word.

*****

James 1:2-4

2 Consider it pure joy, my brothers and sisters, whenever you
face trials of many kinds, 3 because you know that the testing
of your faith produces perseverance. 4 Let perseverance
finish its work so that you may be mature and complete, not
lacking anything.

*****

James 1:12

Blessed is the one who perseveres under trial because, having stood the test, that person will receive the crown of life that the Lord has promised to those who love him.

*****

2 Thessalonians 1:4

Therefore, among God's churches we boast about your perseverance and faith in all the persecutions and trials you are enduring.

*****

Psalm 139:23

Search me, God, and know my heart; test me and know my anxious thoughts.

*****

Psalm 27:14

Wait for the LORD; be strong and take heart
and wait for the LORD.

*****

Psalm 40:1

I waited patiently for the LORD;
he turned to me and heard my cry.

*****

Isaiah 40:31

...but those who hope in the LORD will renew their strength. They will soar on wings like eagles; they will run and not grow weary, they will walk and not be faint.

*****

Isaiah 28:16

So this is what the Sovereign LORD says: "See, I lay a stone in Zion, a tested stone, a precious cornerstone for a sure foundation; the one who relies on it
will never be stricken with panic.

*****

Romans 12:2

Do not conform to the pattern of this world, but be transformed by the renewing of your mind. Then you will be able to test and approve what God's will is—his good, pleasing and perfect will.

*****

Philippians 4:4-9, 11b-13, 19-20

4 Rejoice in the Lord always. I will say it again: Rejoice!
5 Let your gentleness be evident to all. The Lord is near.
6 Do not be anxious about anything, but in every situation,
by prayer and petition, with thanksgiving,
present your requests to God.
7 And the peace of God, which transcends all understanding,
will guard your hearts and your minds in Christ Jesus.
8 Finally, brothers and sisters, whatever is true, whatever is
noble, whatever is right, whatever is pure, whatever is
lovely, whatever is admirable – if anything is excellent or
praiseworthy – think about such things. 9 Whatever you
have learned or received or heard from me, or seen in me –
put it into practice. And the God of peace will be with you.
11b I have learned to be content whatever the circumstances.
12 I know what it is to be in need, and I know what it is to
have plenty. I have learned the secret of being content in any
and every situation, whether well fed or hungry,
whether living in plenty or in want.
13 I can do all this through him who gives me strength.
19 And my God will meet all your needs according to the
riches of his glory in Christ Jesus.
20 To our God and Father be glory for ever and ever. Amen.

*****

Colossians 3:15-17

15 Let the peace of Christ rule in your hearts, since as
members of one body you were called to peace.
And be thankful.
16 Let the message of Christ dwell among you richly as you
teach and admonish one another with all wisdom through
psalms, hymns, and songs from the Spirit, singing to God
with gratitude in your hearts.
17 And whatever you do, whether in word or deed, do it all
in the name of the Lord Jesus, giving thanks to
God the Father through him.

*****

Romans 8:34-37

34 Who then is the one who condemns? No one. Christ Jesus
who died—more than that, who was raised to life—is at the
right hand of God and is also interceding for us.
35 Who shall separate us from the love of Christ? Shall
trouble or hardship or persecution or famine or nakedness
or danger or sword? 36 As it is written:
"For your sake we face death all day long; we are considered
as sheep to be slaughtered."
37 No, in all these things we are more than conquerors
through him who loved us.

*****

2 Corinthians 12:10

That is why, for Christ's sake, I delight in weaknesses, in insults, in hardships, in persecutions, in difficulties. For when I am weak, then I am strong.

*****

Contents

Selected Scripture 7

This Book: An Introduction 19

Contributors 31

Prologue
Crisis Experiences and My Prayer
Tim Woolpert, Singer, Songwriter, Friend 35

Chapter 1
Fear Not During the Storms of Life
Richard A. Redd, M.D.
Author *All-In or Nothing * Master Your Destiny* and *All-In or Nothing * A Guide for Advanced Study of Comprehensive Mastery* 43

Chapter 2
Racism
Pastor Vernon Lintvedt
Blessed Savior Lutheran Church (LCMS), O'Fallon, Illinois 57

Chapter 3
Grief Has No Expiration Date
Terry Burgess
Author *When Our Blue Star Turned Gold* *69*

Chapter 4
At Issue Is Our Schools
Richard A. Redd, M.D. *83*

Chapter 5
Death and Grief
Angela Williams, Contracting Officer,
Federal Government,
Author *Knowing You Have Done Your Best* *99*

Chapter 6
The COVID-19 Pandemic
Hiren Raval, Registered Pharmacist,
Haslet, Texas *103*

Chapter 7
Thoughts on the News Media in Today's Crazy,
Politically Charged Culture
Barry Willey, U.S. Army COL, Retired
Author *Out of the Valley* and
Extreme Investing, *107*

Chapter 8
Compassion and Common Ground for Those
Affected by Crisis
Bud Hendrickson, Industrial Engineering and Maintenance/Management
Author *Enjoy Your Journey: Ten Bedrock Truths to Improve Everything About You* 115

Chapter 9
Content Whatever the Circumstances
John Emra, CEO Life Is Full of Choices
Author *Cornerstones and Core Needs of Growing Kids, Parenting from the Top of the Mountain,* and *Seven Steps to the Top of the Mountain* 127

Chapter 10
Who Is My Neighbor?
James Patton, Former V.P. Operations, Absolute Security 139

Chapter 11
Navigating Uncharted Waters
Sarah S. Falcone,
BSN (Bachelor of Science Nursing), RN;
Christian Yoga Teacher CYT-200;
Home Healthcare Nurse, Fort Worth, Texas;
Medical Reserve Corps of
Tarrant County, Texas 151

Chapter 12
A Spoonful of Cookie Dough
Will Hathaway, Police Officer, Patrol Officer, SWAT (Special Weapons and Tactics) Negotiator, School Resource Officer, Trainer, Part Time Pastor Author *What If God Is Like This? The Human Side of Christ * Meet the Guy Behind the God,* and *Naked* *161*

Chapter 13
Restore the American Dream
Larry Wolf, Department Chair Criminal Justice, University of Antelope Valley, Lancaster, California Author *A Black and White Decision * Why George Zimmerman Was Found Innocent * Why America Must Honor the Memory of Trayvon Martin,* and *Policing Peace: What America Can Do Now to Avoid Future Tragedies* *169*

Chapter 14
Through Extreme Pain and Loss, God Helps Us Endure
Lenny and Grace Belvedere, Owners of Ottavio's Restaurant, Lakeside, California *185*

Chapter 15
When Important Things Fail
Mike Atkinson, Owner/Publisher *Mikey's Funnies* *199*

*****

*****

This Book: An Introduction

The idea behind ***God's Plan Unfolding * Strength and Renewal in Times of Crisis*** is this: the book consists of a collection of true stories, perspectives, and reflections from people in varied walks of life, who, through faith, confronted and handle crises. Many crises affect us and in varied ways. Contributors to the book represent a wide variety of vocations, interests, ethnicity, and age groups. Each contributor has willingly agreed to submit his/her writings.

We celebrate the lives, strengths, and endurance of individuals who have offered their stories and opinions. The context is anchored, at least in part, on the history of the Apostle Paul who, according to Scripture, endured severe trial, testing, and even torment as he preached while embarked on his three missionary journeys and post-conversion.

God's Plan Unfolding * Strength and Renewal in Times of Crisis relates with the events of 2020 at the time of this writing, and other current timelines, including stories of endurance and perseverance from the Bible.

This is *not* a political book; rather, it is a book of faith, humility, endurance, confidence, and reliance on God across many spectrums.

The Apostle Paul, a writer of much of the New Testament, was a man of deep and sincere faith after his conversion. His history projected strong credibility for the people and cultures he addressed throughout the known world, both Jews and non-Jews. He was called by God to be an Apostle after he had persecuted the early church, actions he freely admitted.

What were his credentials and what was his story? In Acts 22:3-5 he is quoted speaking to a Jewish audience: **3**"I am a Jew; born in Tarsus of Cilicia ... I studied under Gamaliel and was thoroughly trained in the law of our ancestors. I was just as zealous for God as any of you are today. **4** I persecuted the followers of this Way [what today we would call Christian believers] to their death, arresting both men and women and throwing them into prison, **5** as the high priest and all the Council can themselves testify. I even obtained letters from them to their associates in Damascus, and went there to bring these people as prisoners to Jerusalem to be punished.

6 "About noon as I came near Damascus, suddenly a bright light from heaven flashed around me. **7** I fell to the ground and heard a voice say to me, 'Saul! Saul! Why do you persecute me?'

8 "'Who are you, Lord?' I asked. "'I am Jesus of Nazareth, whom you are persecuting,' he replied. 9 My companions saw the light, but they did not understand the voice of him who was speaking to me.

10 "'What shall I do, Lord?' I asked.

"'Get up,' the Lord said, 'and go into Damascus. There you will be told all that you have been assigned to do.' 11 My companions led me by the hand into Damascus, because the brilliance of the light had blinded me.

12 "A man named Ananias came to see me. He was a devout observer of the law and highly respected by all the Jews living there. 13 He stood beside me and said, 'Brother Saul, receive your sight!' And at that very moment I was able to see him.

14 "Then he said: 'The God of our ancestors has chosen you to know his will and to see the Righteous One and to hear words from his mouth. 15 You will be his witness to all people of what you have seen and heard. 16 And now what are you waiting for? Get up, be baptized and wash your sins away, calling on his name.'"

Paul possessed a Jewish heritage; he was also a Roman citizen, and he was called to be an Apostle. His background presented credibility. He knew what he was talking about.

His letters to various churches reveal his depth of experiences and understanding.

Paul had experienced a radical conversion. Afterward, he embarked a mission that would take him through much of the known world, to preach the gospel and proclaim the truth of Jesus.

According to his own account, he was not a "trained" speaker (2 Corinthians 11:6). While obeying his calling, that which God had commanded him to do, he was severely treated, often beaten, and chained (Acts 26; Philippians 1:12). He was put in prison. He experienced a shipwreck and predicted, accurately, that none of the passengers would be lost. He suffered much for what he believed (Romans 5:3). Indeed, his sacrifice for the cause of Christ was painful, and eventually led to his death. He did not falter through suffering for a righteous cause. He endured.

Why reference the Apostle Paul, his Godly mission to spread the truth of the gospel, and the accompanying sufferings he endured about which he wrote, offering examples of reliance on God and endurance through storms as he commanded the exercise of personal responsibility? I'll tell you why: because many believers currently, though not Apostles in a literal sense, have become inundated with negative influences from a myriad of sources; some are discouraged, deeply distraught; others have suffered for their religious beliefs, and still others for their defense of their country, in this case, the United States of America.

As of the time of this writing, millions are consistently exposed to incessant and ever-changing media news coverage. Many have endured harmful stresses including illnesses from the virus, COVID-19, and in some cases, the deaths of friends and family; they have been subjected to quarantines, financial losses from "lockdowns," closing of churches and businesses, and layoffs. Stark divisions of opinion have risen, seemingly unabated. Threats abound as does "silence" when it comes to choosing not to express opinions that may not "fit" a so-called mainstream view, for fear of retaliation. Worry and fear abound to various degrees.

A few knowledgeable friends, whom I respect, have even questioned whether America can survive all of this in 2020 and beyond. Many pastors I have heard say they have never seen anything like what we see and endure in their lifetimes. While not a pastor, I agree with that conclusion. For as long as I have been alive, I have never witnessed the degrees of stress and hostility constantly observed.

In spite of all of this, we endeavor to keep going. We choose to let our faith in God be our guide as to how to react, and we resolve to remain true and faithful to the causes of justice, mercy, forgiveness, and most of all, love, investing encouragement, grace, faith, and truth in one another.

America was founded on Biblical principles and practices, as any study of true American history shows. We agree with **WallBuilders**. According to Google: "WallBuilders is an organization dedicated to presenting America's forgotten history and heroes, with an emphasis on the moral, religious, and constitutional foundation on which America was built—a foundation which, in recent years, has been seriously attacked and undermined. In accord with what was so accurately stated by George Washington, we believe that 'the propitious [favorable] smiles of heaven can never be expected on a nation which disregards the eternal rules of order and right which heaven itself has ordained.'"

This book is written as a renewed call to faith and revival, asking, even imploring God to intervene in dramatic ways, praying for our leaders regardless of political party, and loving those with whom we may disagree, earnestly desiring, praying, and believing for Divine intervention and protection, and to sustain and encourage those who may be disheartened now, praying for God's peace to rule and reign.

The Apostle Paul said this:

"No, in all these things we are more than conquerors
through him who loved us."
Romans 8:37

In High School, many years ago, I had a youth pastor who made an indelible impression on me. He explained that verse like this, and likely the explanation was not his own: "'More than conquerors' means we have not only won the war, but have enough ammunition to fight another battle."

I don't believe and am not saying we are at "war" in a literal sense, though many have uttered the phrase "civil war" in describing hot spots of unrest where civilians have "warred" against each other, including exercising property destruction, violence, and rising crime. My home town of La Mesa, California, was an example in summer, 2020.

I am a student of America's Civil War fought from 1861-1865; at this point I can say we are not there, thankfully! We should be able to disagree, if needed, and do so peacefully.

God's Plan Unfolding * Strength and Renewal in Times of Crisis is a book of faith, endurance, and encouragement from a Biblical point of view. So much division we have witnessed seems to stem from political differences and disagreements, and the question arises, "How do we deal with philosophical and often literal attacks on beliefs and the Constitution of the United States?" Our Constitution has been trampled on, *especially* the First Amendment. The First Amendment says, "Congress shall make no law respecting an establishment of religion, or prohibiting the free exercise thereof; or abridging the freedom of speech, or of the press; or the right of the people peaceably to assemble, and to petition the Government for a redress of grievances." Where and how often has the First Amendment been debased and violated recently and in current history?

Basic human dignity has waned. Showing courtesy and respect when opposing points of view are approached have become rarer. One notable friend recently said, and I agree: "We must *listen* to each other more." Listen and absorb opinions gracefully before we react. Preach it. Listening to you or anyone with respect means I care enough to want to pay attention to your perspectives out of courtesy, grace, and a willingness to learn.

One recurring issue, unfortunately, is the problem of remaining, grossly disrespectful, and prejudicial racism. Conflicts illustrative of this fact have been observed and well-documented on national news. In several cases, murder was the result. As regards race, I am White and one of my dearest friends is Black. We have known each other for well over 30 years. We love each other as brothers today as we did when we first met, and he has a chapter in this book. (James Patton)

Another contributor addresses racial division, and he, too, is a dear friend. He references the George Floyd murder (May 25, 2020), and deals plainly with this awful issue of racism, its dysfunctions and inequities, and proposes God-birthed solutions. (Vern Lintvedt)

Both of these men also provide Biblically based solutions. And in my view, their solutions are scriptural and right.

In some cases, the very existence of law enforcement itself was questioned. Divisions between "Defund the Police" and "Defend the Police" arrested our attention. This fact is addressed in the comments of one of our contributors. (Larry Wolf) He is a university professor of Criminal Justice, a retired sheriff, as well as a committed Christian.

As of this writing, July-September of 2020, America had witnessed and experienced disastrous and devastating events. There is no question about that. Unrest had become the order of the day. Freedoms of expression, religious liberty, and voting rights and methods had been threatened or refused, ostensibly in the name of public health protection. Some of those health protection and virus-spread concerns, to a point, were valid.

We all know that the existence of the COVID-19 virus was real. One dear friend, who works for a hospital in Southern California, verified the risk and sad results as the number of bodies removed due to death from the virus each day was growing in the early part of 2020. That fact was not political – that fact was reality.

There is a brighter side. We have so appreciated frontline health care workers! We honor them! We have heard and experienced stories of great sacrifice of those who have treated others who had contracted COVID-19. While many patients across the country had died, many others had beaten it. We continue to hear conflicting reports of numbers of cases, causes of death. Indeed, we may not have known who or what to believe. (How many times had I heard that from people across many spectrums!)

Here is a bottom line: when trial, testing, lawlessness, worry, fear, and bad news come, including the loss of loved ones to death regardless of cause, we can and must continue to rely on God to sustain us. We also must continue to strive to exercise necessary precautions, in balance whenever a crisis strikes.

As believers, we must showcase Christ's love while remaining true and firm in our principles and practices according to the Bible. Even in the darkest and bleakest of circumstances, there is hope in the Lord. "In God We Trust" – is more than a phrase imprinted on our coins. One friend, endeavoring to "quote" God in a light-hearted moment, said that if he thought God possessed a business card, that card would have printed on one side: "I'm God." On the reverse: "You are not." So true. God is our Sovereign Lord. We are His creation.

This book was written to tell true stories of inspiration, hope, dedication, and truth, and to celebrate God's goodness no matter what difficult and pressing circumstances are being faced. In ***God's Plan Unfolding * Strength and Renewal in Times of Crisis*** you will read the stories and views of people who care deeply about faith, hope, love, America, and you.

You will also share the commitment to God's peace reigning in our hearts and lives.

Trust in God. He never fails. He is always true. We pray and long for His Divine Intervention as individuals, and for individuals, families, organizations, and government.

May you be encouraged as you read ... that is the primary purpose of this author and our contributors who have helped make the book a reality.

We desire to offer this prayer, following the injunction in 2 Chronicles 7:14:

> If my people, who are called by my name, will humble themselves and pray and seek my face and turn from their wicked ways, then I will hear from heaven, and I will forgive their sin and will heal their land.

Our prayer: "God of the Bible, Sovereign Lord, we love You. We humble ourselves before You. Thank You for sending Your Son to teach us, and love us, and gift us salvation through faith and grace. He was One who lived a holy and blameless life, enduring death on a cross, and after His Resurrection He sent His Holy Spirit as a Teacher and Comforter. We seek You. We desire to turn from wickedness, and request Your forgiveness. We are eternally grateful for your gifts of grace, faith, and love. We seek to serve You in all our ways.

"May Your peace begin and flourish in us as a comfort to our persons, and as a witness to others. Encourage us with Your presence. Give us Your hope. We yearn and pray for Your Divine Intervention. Amen."

Contributors

Mike Atkinson, Owner and Publisher of ***Mikey's Funnies,*** a free, week-day clean humor email to thousands of subscribers, generously hosted by www.agathongroup.com; please see www.mikeysfunnies.com

Lenny and Grace Belvedere, Owners, Ottavio's Restaurant, Lakeside, California

Terry Burgess, Author: ***When Our Blue Star Turned Gold***

Mark A. Chrysler, Electrical Inspection Consultant,
San Diego Gas & Electric
Author: ***Authentic Hope * Experiencing God's Presence Even When You Are an Unwilling Participant * "Living Life with a Footnote"***

John Emra, CEO Life Is Full of Choices
Author: ***Cornerstones and Core Needs of Growing Kids, Parenting from the Top of the Mountain,*** and
Seven Steps to the Top of the Mountain

Sarah S. Falcone, BSN (Bachelor of Science Nursing), RN; Certified Yoga Teacher YTT-200; Home Healthcare Nurse, Fort Worth, Texas; Medical Reserve Corps of Tarrant County, Texas; FEMA Volunteer

Will Hathaway, Police Officer, Patrol Officer,
SWAT (Special Weapons and Tactics) Negotiator,
School Resource Officer, Trainer, Part Time Pastor
Author: ***What If God Is Like This?, The Human Side of Christ * Meet the Guy Behind The God,*** and ***Naked***

Everett (Bud) Hendrickson, Industrial Engineering and Maintenance Management
Author: ***Enjoy Your Journey * Ten Bedrock Truths to Improve Everything About You***

Pastor Vernon Lintvedt, Blessed Savior Lutheran Church (LCMS), O'Fallon, Illinois

James Patton, Former V.P. Operations, Absolute Security

Hiren Raval, Pharmacist, Haslet, Texas

Rick Redd, MD, U.S. Army COL, Retired
Author: ***All-In or Nothing * Master Your Destiny * Achieve Excellence in Sport and Life,*** U.S. Army COL, Retired

Barry Willey, U.S. Army COL, Retired, former Public Affairs Officer (PAO)
Author: ***Out of the Valley*** and ***Extreme Investing***

Angela Williams, Contracting Officer, United States Federal Government
Author: ***Knowing You Have Done Your Best * No Regrets***

Larry Wolf, Los Angeles County Sheriff, Retired, Department Chair, Criminal Justice, University of Antelope Valley, Lancaster, California
Author: ***A Black and White Decision * Why George Zimmerman Was Found Innocent * Why America Must Honor the Memory of Trayvon Martin***, and ***Policing Peace: What America Can Do Now to Avoid Future Tragedies***

Tim Woolpert, Singer, Songwriter, Friend

Prologue
Crisis Experiences and My Prayer

Tim Woolpert, Singer, Songwriter, Friend
August 25, 2020

I have witnessed too many tragedies in my life, most of which were death related. Not so many family and friends, but strangers. These were not outcomes of war or conflict ... well, not a war that was driven by any government ... rather, an everyday reality where I grew up.

I thought I had become desensitized to death and its emotions. One night when I was fifteen, I heard gunshots ring out around at 3:00 a.m. and I ran out my back door to look over my fence just in time to see two young men I recognized from the hood. They were running by; of course, I saw nothing, but that is another reality.

Once the smoke cleared and the police were on scene, I went out to see the carnage. As they helped one victim up who was apparently just pistol whipped, I made my way around the police tape and across the street to talk to a friend who was awakened as well by the violence. I made my way between two parked cars, and that is when I saw the young man lying there clinging to life. I will never forget the look of fear he had as we locked eyes.

I yelled for the police, and as they made their way over, he had reached up and grabbed my hand. I knelt beside him trying to encourage life, telling him to hold on and everything was going to be okay.

The whole time my grip increased while his diminished. The police and paramedics came in all around me and because of the position we were in, I could not retreat. They cut his shirt and pants off. There was no blood, just two black holes. One in his stomach and one in his chest, apparently point-blank shots.

He started shaking and his breathing became shallow and labored. I called to my friend to grab a blanket for him, and the chills ran down my spine when the paramedic responded with "Don't waste your time." I never once lost eye contact with the young man that had chosen me to help him fix this, to make it go away. I just held his hand and stared into his eyes. I can only describe the end like this: he tried to take a couple last deep breaths, but was unable to get any air into his lungs and he went from looking at me, to looking through me, and that would haunt me to this day.

I am 50 now and I can still see his face like it was yesterday. Again, I had seen many deaths on those streets, but none as real as the seventeen-year-old boy I watched die that night. I did not know then that this would not be the crisis that would define me. It was not until many years later when I would have to deal with the loss of a life much greater, the death of my mother. My mother and I were extremely close, best friends close. My mom was 5′ nothing and 90 pounds soaking wet, and when it came to her babies, she was a lioness, and no harm was going to come to her cubs. She was my world.

I called her one night after she had some dental surgery to check on her. She was in tears because of the pain. I told her to take her pain medication as prescribed and get some sleep, and that I would call her in the morning. Much like every other conversation we had, she always had one more thing to say and we talked another fifteen minutes. The next morning was like any other morning: I got up at zero dark thirty and made my way to the oil fields. My older brother was working as my hand on the rig and was with me for the mindless zombie-like trek we made every day.

After a couple hours of working, my phone rang and it was my stepfather asking to speak with my brother. He put the phone to his ear and his face immediately changed to a look of panic and despair. My brother kept repeating the word "What!!!" over and over. With blank face he hung up the phone as he began to well up, and without a word I just knew. I said, "Mom's dead." I couldn't breathe, I couldn't think, I couldn't speak. I was just numb.

We shut down the rig and made the hour-long drive back in just under thirty minutes. We arrived at her house. My stepfather was out front with the police, waiting on the coroner. I began to enter and an officer stopped me and said that I would not be permitted to do so. I gestured with my arms to handcuff me, as I was not taking no for an answer. This was still not real, and I had to see her. He finally conceded and instructed me to touch nothing. My brother waited outside; he has never dealt with loss very well. I entered the living room through the kitchen and could see her feet through the doorway ahead. I will never forget the deafening silence in that house. I turned the corner and there she was, on the floor, covered with a blanket.

Nothing in my life has ever been as real and final as that moment. I uncovered her because I had to see for myself what was not yet reality in my mind, and there she was, "My Everything" ... gone. There were signs of aspiration around her mouth and she did not look completely at peace. The thing that bothered me most outside of her passing was that her toes were curled so tightly, like it hurt; and that would be burned in my mind forever.

I sat beside her for a while until I was instructed to exit the room. My mom wore a lot of jewelry, not expensive, but it was her jewelry. At the risk of anything disappearing, I removed it before exiting and put it in a box on her mantle. I do not know why; I just felt like she would want me to.

The coroner arrived moments later and after some time inside, they wheeled "My Everything" by me on a gurney in a body bag. My life had changed forever. Almost immediately, I became emotionally bankrupt as it pertained to tragedy and any crisis for that matter.

In my world no one will ever feel the degree of pain or the sense of loss I felt. My stepfather had a different solution to dealing with this crisis, and chose to take his own life a couple months later as he became convinced that her loss was more than God had given him the strength to endure.

To this day when friends or acquaintances discuss losing someone they love, I can only empathize; my sympathy unfortunately died that day with my mother. My father passed away six years later from yet another unforeseen tragedy. He was on his roof adjusting the antenna when he lost his balance and fell to the ground landing on his head. I was at the hospital with him and made the decision to take him off life support as had been instructed by him in life.

This would be the second person I would watch die while I held his hand.

I pray to God every day to fix me, but instead He gives me the strength to endure.

I pray to God every day to fix me, but instead He gives me the strength to endure.

Always say I love you, and never go to bed angry.

From Tim 08-26-20: *Glen, these are the lyrics to a song I wrote for my mother after she passed. It was recorded on our 6th album, but never performed live.*

Faded

Yesterday seems a million miles away
Can't erase our last embrace I miss you
Don't cry I just drown all the pain inside
Won't go away just want to say I love you
Not my fault but there's nobody left to blame
Life goes on without you
Not fair want to call and you won't be there
Sometimes seems it's not true
So lost am I never to find my way
Scream but no one hears me
Feel abandoned as I live in denial I pray
Oh God please come fix me
At night lay awake and I see your face
A special moment that the darkness will soon replace
I comfort others just despite my pain
I can't deal with mine I know it's time I started
Everybody deals with things in a different way
My brother cries and my sister she cuts the pain
Just want to hold them let them know it'll be okay
It's hard to heal how others feel I'm broken
You left behind something time cannot replace
Endless sea of sorrow
Oh, my God, I miss you more it seems everyday

Afraid to face tomorrow
Emptiness you'll forever be missed
And I wish I could just hold you
One more time just to say my goodbyes
And all the things I never told you
Can God hear my cries
When I pray at night
To take my pain away make me whole again
My heart's an open book for all to read
The pages faded now
Almost empty
Why do we love when we know that we have to lose
Everything explain to me it's pointless
I want to heal but still I'm afraid to feel
Anything that's left of me I'm hopeless
Don't want to cry because I don't want to feel the pain
I just pray for closure
I tell myself that you've gone to a better place
I know that now for sure
I'll see you later so I never will say goodbye
Always here inside me
For life till the day that I die
I know you'll be there to guide me
Can God hear my cries
When I pray at night
To take my pain away make me whole again
My hearts an open book for all to read
The pages faded now
Almost empty

Dear mother, you're home with God, so spread your wings
Finally rest in peace I'll take care of things
I'll always love you and I know you'll see
I'll do my best in life to make you proud of me…

*****

Author's Note: **Tim Woolpert** and I have been close friends for well over twenty years. When I was consulting with his firm and other similar firms in the area, consisting of construction, oil, and building contractor businesses, we formed a solid friendship. At its core, our friendship was defined by mutual respect, music (though experienced in very different styles from each other), shared local dining experiences which included loads of laughter, and most of all, genuine heartfelt care. Tim is a brilliant thinker, a problem-solver, and innovator, a poet. I learned early on the deep loss Tim was able and felt free to share about losing his mother—and you can see in this chapter and poem that losing his mom was a crisis for him; the pain and memories remain. For a man, now 50, who has lived with more than his fair share of losses, he is absolutely correct to credit God with the strength to endure. *This choice is what this book is all about.* In any crisis, no matter the severity, we can trust God to sustain us because He cares. Read on and experience the stories of others. Be encouraged as you grow in faith and resilience, relying on God's love for you and those around you.

Chapter 1
Fear Not During the Storms of Life

Richard A. Redd, MD, U.S. Army COL, Retired
Author
All-In or Nothing * Master Your Destiny and
All-In or Nothing * A Guide for Advanced Study of Comprehensive Mastery

September 7, 2020

> Matthew 8:23-27
> 23 Then he got into the boat and his disciples
> followed him. 24 Suddenly a furious storm
> came up on the lake, so that the waves swept
> over the boat. But Jesus was sleeping. 25The
> disciples went and woke him, saying, "Lord,
> save us! We're going to drown!" 26 He replied,
> "You of little faith, why are you so afraid?"
> Then he got up and rebuked the winds and the
> waves, and it was completely calm. 27 The men
> were amazed and asked, "What kind of man is
> this? Even the winds and the waves obey him!"

Who do you believe and in whom do you trust when the storms of life are raging, and you are in dire need of help or encouragement? Who is your infallible source of insight or information when you have an unexpected accident, the acute onset of an illness, or you lose your job? Do you turn to a family member or a loyal friend? Maybe you look to the government as the "fixer" of all things, or science, or medicine. Maybe you find comfort in the philosophy books. How is that working out for you? Do you find solace in those sources?

For me, there is only one Source of true comfort when life deals me an unexpected blow, and that is God. I adhere to the principle that there are no accidents in life. Everything happens for a reason. We may not always know why, but we can rest resolutely in the fact that God is knitting all things together for our good, without exception. Only He is all-knowing, present everywhere, and all-powerful. He controls your destiny and mine, not your boss, your spouse, the politicians, or the financial markets.

Do you believe that? Do you have faith that God is unequivocally sovereign in your life? If not, why not? Giving Him control of your life is a simple matter. All that is necessary is to humbly ask Him to forgive the mistakes you have made and will continue to make as you go forward (Romans 3:10, 23 and Romans 10:13), believe in Jesus (John 3:16 and John 1:12), and then give Him the reins of your life (Romans 10:9-10). You can do this anywhere and anytime.

If you do believe that God is in control, why can it be so hard to live in accordance with that belief? We should be exuberant, grateful, bold and fearless. Instead, we sometimes doubt and we struggle. I had to deal with this issue personally during the COVID-19 pandemic of 2020.

During the early phases of the pandemic, I listened to the "experts" and the political leaders, as they pontificated about the virus and its possible effect on the people of this country. At first, I relied on their expertise and their experience, and I earnestly believed that they would hold the best interest of the country foremost in their minds. Policies were instituted (travel restrictions, sheltering in place) as we fought to "flatten the curve" and mitigate the disease. As the weeks went by schools, churches and business were closed.

As the pandemic stretched from weeks to months, many mistakes were made. That is not unusual, and is understandable in many ways, because it was a new virus and it behaved in ways that were slightly different from others we had encountered in the past. As the issue became more politicized, though, distortions were made and people were hurt. I am not wise enough to ascertain the motives behind these actions. I only saw the fruit that they bore.

I probably should have turned off the television and the radio (where I was getting most of my information), turned to the Lord, busied myself with a worthwhile project and waited until the storm had passed. I was getting angry because people were dying, and I didn't understand why. Medical precepts I had been taught were being violated. I can say, in retrospect, that the anger I felt was counter-productive for me (increased stress, increased blood pressure, lower quality sleep) and had absolutely no effect of the situation at hand. The issue was clearly outside my circle of influence, though it was still a matter of concern.

My niece called in the spring of 2020, and asked for my opinion about the virus. She is the mother of a 12-year old, and was curious to know what she could do to help protect herself, her husband, and her child. For her, the "politics" was all local and practical. I wanted to be helpful and optimistic, so I shared with her what I am about to tell you without any emotional or political overtones. "Just the facts, sir."

What do we know about the coronavirus as of September, 2020?

1. The actual name of this virus is SARS-CoV-2. This stands for Sudden Acute Respiratory Syndrome coronavirus-2. COVID-19 is the disease that it causes and the name of the pandemic; the 19 means that it started in 2019 (December 30, 2019 to be exact).
2. This virus originated in Wuhan, China. Whether it came from bats in an open market or from a viral laboratory has yet to be determined.
3. The coronavirus is a class of viruses which includes a common cold virus (least deadly) up to and including the SARS virus (most deadly).
4. It is an RNA virus, like influenza, HIV, measles, mumps, rabies, and polio.

5. 99.8% of the people who are infected with coronavirus are either asymptomatic or have minimal symptoms.
6. The death rate is 0.26%, slightly higher than the flu.
7. Human-to-human transmission of the virus was confirmed on January 20, 2020.
8. The coronavirus is spread in three primary ways:
   a. Respiratory droplets from coughing, sneezing, laughing, or singing out to a distance of six feet.
   b. Indirect contact. The virus may remain viable (alive) on copper for four hours, cardboard for one day, and on plastic and stainless steel for up to 3 days.
   c. Direct contact. Since the virus is carried in the nasopharynx, touching someone's face or hugging/kissing them may spread the disease.
9. The virus is killed by soap, antiseptics (60% alcohol), and UV radiation.
10. The incubationary period (time from infection to onset of symptoms) will vary depending on the number of viruses one is exposed to (viral load) and the susceptibility of the patient. Those patients with a suppressed immune system are likely to manifest disease sooner and more significantly. The average incubation period is two to ten days, but has been as long as twenty-one days.
11. In most patients, the virus itself is not the cause of death. It is the response of the patient to the virus that is lethal. If the immune system over-responds to the virus, a condition known as cytokine storm arises. An

outpouring of powerful inflammatory proteins occurs which causes the lungs, liver, kidneys, heart, and other vital organs to shut down.

12. Coronavirus gains access to the body through the respiratory tract. It attacks specific cells in the lungs (alveolar II pneumocytes), and pneumonia can develop.
13. Patients initially present with fever, cough, and shortness of breath. Some patients have fatigue, body aches, headache, and an inability to taste or smell.
14. Each viral particle (viron) is much less than one micron in size (the normal red blood cell is seven microns in diameter).
15. Many strains of the virus are known to exist, much like the influenza virus. Like the flu virus, as the coronavirus mutates, a different vaccine will have to be produced and administered each year to be protective.

Most people are unaware of the fact that pathogens (bacteria, fungi, viruses, and parasites) are ubiquitous; they are around us and within us every day. We breathe them into our lungs and ingest them into our gut regularly. In other words, all of us are routinely being "exposed" to these pathogens. Perhaps "colonized" is a more accurate word. Most of the time we never know that we have been colonized, and most of the time we don't get ill. Our immune systems are strong enough to fight off any which threaten to do us harm.

Recent discoveries in gut research have shown that we live at peace and in conjunction with 100 trillion bacteria and other microbes (some of which are viruses) which take up residence in our gastrointestinal tract from the mouth to the rectum. These organisms are indispensable to human life; they protect us against harmful pathogens, help us break down food to release energy, and produce vitamins for our daily use.

Many times we are infected with a pathogen which causes little symptoms, but it finds a home within our bodies. Cytomegalovirus has been found in the atheromatous plaque in the arteries of older people. Those of us who have fever blisters harbor the herpes simplex 1 virus (HSV-1) in our nervous systems (dorsal root ganglia). When activated by various triggers (sunlight, stress for example), these viruses reignite and erupt on the skin as painful blisters. Otherwise they lie dormant within us.

There is much about viruses and the science of virology that we are just learning. New discoveries are being made every month of every year.

The coronavirus, like any other virus, can be deadly to those people who are most at risk. This seems to be those over 70 years of age with other medical problems (obesity, high blood pressure, heart disease, lung disease, diabetes). Nursing home patients are particularly vulnerable.

Now that we know something about the virus, what can be done to protect us and to lessen its effect should we be exposed? Here are some action steps you might consider taking:

1. Pray regularly, asking God for wisdom to do the things most prudent to keep you and your loved ones safe.
2. Pray for our political leaders.
3. Look daily for answers in Scripture.
4. Arm yourself with facts about the situation from reliable, trustworthy sources. I honestly believe that gathering relevant, truthful facts about an issue, like COVID-19, is important in trying to understand it and deal with it. It makes sense that the more we know, if truthful, the more helpful we can be to others, and the more we can allay our own fears about what the future may hold. We can then choose to act or not to act in accordance with what we have learned and the policies which have been laid down by our political leaders.
    a. If you are in a high-risk group, limit your exposure to others who are ill.
    b. Wear a mask or shield when you are in close proximity to others, especially if it makes you feel more protected. I find that the shield is much more tolerable and less confining than the tightly-fitting mask.
    c. Wash your hands regularly with soap and water; washing time should be a minimum of twenty seconds.

   d. Refrain from touching your face with your hands.
   e. Spend as much time outdoors as the weather allows.
5. Choose to be positive and happy. There is much to be thankful for. Remember, God is in control of everything that occurs or does not occur.
6. If you are watching television or listening to the radio, choose people and programs who lift your spirits and encourage your forward movement.
7. Strengthen your own immunity in order to fight this virus, but also other pathogens which will inevitably come along (colds, flu). Options for doing this include:
   a. Eating a healthy, well-balanced diet
   b. Eat organic fruits and vegetables (free of pesticides and herbicides) and meat and dairy (free of antibiotics and hormones) whenever possible.
   c. Avoid added sugars and high fructose corn syrup. Look at the package label to see if these are present, and in what quantities. If either are placed first or second in the list of ingredients, put the package back on the shelf.
   d. Focus on carbohydrates, such as starches and fiber. They are found in whole grains, vegetables, and legumes (beans). These are helpful carbohydrates which generate glucose for energy, but also have a low glycemic index (absorption rate into the body) so they do not cause spikes in insulin (good!).
   e. The ideal mixture of macronutrients (carbohydrates, proteins, and fats) in your diet

should be low carbs (20-30%), intermediate proteins (30-40%) and the balance in healthy fats (saturated, monounsaturated, and polyunsaturated fats). Avoid an excess of omega 6 fatty acids and all trans fats. This diet is obviously different from the low-fat, high carb diet which has been recommended by dieticians, the medical community, and the government, and which has led to epidemics in obesity and Type II diabetes over the past 50 years.

f. Consider intermittent fasting (24-30 hours twice a week) as opposed to calorie reduction/restriction diets. Fasting is very effective in resetting your metabolic and hormonal thermostat in order to keep you healthy.
g. During your fasts, stay well hydrated with water, tea, or coffee. Adequate hydration is also very important when you are eating normally. Drink enough so that you are urinating every 2-3 hours.
h. Uninterrupted sleep for 7-8 hours per night is key to restoration and recovery of our mental agility.
i. Take supplementary vitamins and minerals, vitamin D3, CoQ10 (ubiquinol), magnesium, and vitamin C to keep your body and your immune system tuned up.
j. Get moderate daily exercise, including strength-building, flexibility, and aerobic exercise. This could be walking, martial arts or self-defense training, or anything you enjoy doing.

8. Take steps to prevent accidents around your house (falls especially). An injury will divert energy and resources from your immune system to your musculoskeletal system in order to heal.
9. Learn something new every day.
10. Continue to reach out and maintain contact with friends and loved ones, even if you cannot be with them. Facetime, texting, email, letters help keep those lines of support and communication open.
11. When you speak with others, encourage them in the Lord. Share what you have been learning in order to encourage them. There is no benefit in being negative, and no downside to being positive—*no matter* what the situation is.

There are things you can do to lessen your chances of being ill. You are never helpless, and God is always on your side.

Make it a point to make the most of a pandemic or any crisis. While others fiddle, redeem the time! Elevate yourself and your family. Seek the Lord. We had been given time to think, to contemplate, and to plan. The pace of life had slowed, if only briefly, and we didn't know how long it would be before it would ramp up again (I am confident that it must). What else would you like to do with your life?

Are there other jobs or vocations you would like to pursue? What has God been whispering about to you in your ear? What lessons do you want to teach your children or grandchildren? Is there a book you've always wanted to read? Is there a hobby (piano, painting) you would like to try? Would you like to learn to speak Spanish or German? What about that on-line American history or civics course you have wanted to take? Maybe it is time to plant that garden you've always wanted.

I could not encourage you enough to *just do it!*

Perhaps you will open up a part of the world you never thought was possible. You may look back on 2020 as the beginning of your new and exciting life—the one you had always dreamed about. It reminds me of the story of Joseph in the Bible, a man who was sold into slavery by his brothers. Through diligence, hard-work, and honesty, Joseph became a very powerful official in Egypt, second only to Pharaoh. When famine occurred, Joseph was in a position to rescue his family and save them from starvation. Joseph's brothers meant to harm him; God meant it all for good.

For more information on maximizing your health, read more about the twenty-one healthy habits to master your destiny and more than 30 ways to implement them in my book, *All-In or Nothing*. It is available through my website, www.all-inornothing.com, or through Amazon or Barnes & Noble.

Sometimes God leads us into the wilderness. The healthiest and most beneficial thing we can do is keep the faith, rest beneath His mighty wing, and do the things He has taught us to do. He has never let us down, and He never will. If you are tempted to be fearful and murmur, remember that God already has the situation under His perfect control.

Go forth, and do well.
God speed.

*****

Author's Note: **Rick Redd, MD** has a rich history. As an author, he is a referral from one of our other authors, Bob Dees. In fact, Bob Dees, Rick Redd, and Barry Willey, all published authors with Creative Team Publishing, were in the same class at West Point (United States Military Academy, New York). He is an international champion shooter, along with being a medical doctor with a true, balanced, holistic, and nutrition-sensitive approach. He has years of experience and practical knowledge. He is a man of faith in God. He is one of the most effective physicians I have ever known. I can't recommend strongly enough: Please secure his book and accompanying study guide to experience a proper and Godly motivation for achieving excellence in your chosen endeavor, obtain solid advice on developing and practicing good habits, and to improve your lifestyle and entire life overall.
Please visit this website to learn more and to purchase his books: **www.all-inornothing.com**

Chapter 2
Racism

Pastor Vernon Lintvedt
Blessed Savior Lutheran Church (LCMS), O'Fallon, Illinois

Sermon Script, June 28, 2020

I'd like talk to you this morning about a subject that is relevant to our times and very sensitive. The subject is Racism. I know you've been hearing a lot on the news and seeing images that are too painful to look at. Put those images together with the coronavirus and you feel like you're trapped. I know what those who have been on the oppressed side of racism would say: "If you think the last month has been tiring, try being trapped for 400 years." The temptation to turn off your Holy Spirit hearing aids may be strong but I pray you'll stay with me.

If there is any good that has come out of the George Floyd murder, it may be that we have been forced into this conversation about racism. Sad to say, that is not the only sin listed in the Bible, and like the other Commandments, the complete removal and eradication of racism, just like other sins, will only be accomplished in heaven. Jesus predicted that when he said, "In the last days nation will rise up against nation." I know that sounds pretty defeating.

And that doesn't mean we've been given the right to ignore the subject. Or suggest we should just learn to live with it until the Judgment. The Scriptures are clear that all sin needs to be ferreted out and put to death. That's the struggle every sinner will have to endure till Jesus comes. It is the calling of every serious Christian to work toward ridding oneself of all the acts of the sinful nature. And there are many. And that process can be overwhelming. Nevertheless, as Children of the heavenly Father, we willingly do the work of putting away sinful deeds, for He has removed the judgment we deserve and placed it upon His One and Only Son, Jesus. And to help us in this sanctifying work, God has poured out His love through the Holy Spirit so that we might take on the image of His beloved Son, and learn to live in peace with each other.

I pray God to help me in the next few minutes to handle this painful subject with a large dose of humility and repentance, with the hope that we will all be able to join the praise of King David who wrote in Psalm 96, (NRVS):

> 1 O sing to the LORD a new song; sing to the LORD, all the earth! 2 Sing to the LORD, bless his name; tell of his salvation from day to day. 3 Declare his glory among the nations, his marvelous works among all the peoples.

One of the most important aspects of Christianity which I have used to bring the Gospel to people of different racial or ethnic backgrounds is the fact that Christianity is a religion for all people. Christianity doesn't belong to just Americans or people living in what we call the West. From the beginning of Jesus' ministry, He let be known He was there for the salvation of the world.

Many religions established their "gods" locally and remained a localized religion. Christianity, on the other hand, being established within Judaism, was from the beginning a religion to free all people from sin. Some of the heroes from the stories of Jesus were from enemy territories. You know well the story of the Good Samaritan. But do you remember the story of the Roman Centurion (in Luke, Chapter 7)? The story is set in Capernaum, the home base for Jesus' ministry operations. Luke writes,

> There a centurion's servant, whom his master valued highly, was sick and about to die. [3] The centurion heard of Jesus and sent some elders of the Jews to him, asking him to come and heal his servant. [4] When they came to Jesus, they pleaded earnestly with him, "This man deserves to have you do this, [5] because he loves our nation and has built our synagogue." [6] So Jesus went with them.
>
> He was not far from the house when the centurion sent friends to say to him: "Lord, don't trouble

yourself, for I do not deserve to have you come under my roof. [7] That is why I did not even consider myself worthy to come to you. But say the word, and my servant will be healed. [8] For I myself am a man under authority, with soldiers under me. I tell this one, 'Go,' and he goes; and that one, 'Come,' and he comes. I say to my servant, 'Do this,' and he does it."

[9] When Jesus heard this, he was amazed at him, and turning to the crowd following him, he said, "I tell you, I have not found such great faith even in Israel." [10] Then the men who had been sent returned to the house and found the servant well.

It is clear from this story and others like it, that Jesus had targeted His grace on people outside the chosen people of Israel. Jesus told Nicodemus, "God so loved the World that He gave His only Son."

Jesus was doing the task that God had given to Israel who was supposed to be a magnet for God, so that when those throughout the world saw how God treated this special people, they too would be drawn to Him. Unfortunately, they failed in their mission and became exclusive like so many other religions. That's a temptation the church must face in our world today.

Christianity has always had a view toward redeeming all people, and the book of Revelation pictures the throne of God in heaven as a place where all the saints are gathered from every tribe and nation. Before Jesus ascended into heaven, 40 days after His resurrection, He gave His disciples this mission... "you will receive power when the Holy Spirit has come upon you, and you will be my witnesses in Jerusalem and in all Judea and Samaria, and to the end of the earth." How does that work in our world today? Are we buying into that same mission created by our Lord?

I believe most of us think we are pretty open people, even bias-free. But let me ask you, "Have you ever given another person 'The Look' that suggested you were leery of their intentions only because of their skin color and not because you knew of any intent to do something unlawful or harmful?" I have. And upon further contemplation I have asked myself, "Where did that come from?"

Was it because I caught a glimpse of the Chicago riots back in 1968? Or was it the big High School basketball game my high school had with an All-Black inner-city school in San Diego where a serious fight broke out after the game. Our vice principal was knocked unconscious with a pipe concealed in an umbrella. Those were tumultuous times to be sure. But mixed in with those memories, are really good recollections of people of color who were my friends.

One of the kids I grew up with, of African-American ancestry, was the son of a Judge. His name was Sean. He was not only on our football team but a wonderful Christian young man. During my college years, I worked for a manager of a grocery store who during our lunch hour gave me a Master's Course on Black Classical Vocalists. I was a little embarrassed that I didn't know any of them and I was supposedly majoring in music. Some of you may remember a man I considered to be one of the greatest Gospel Singers/Evangelists in the world back in the 1960s and 70s.

I met Andraé Crouch when I was in High School and he became my friend. He used to call me and invite me to recording sessions when I was living in LA. He was a five-time Grammy-award winning composer, who preached Christ unapologetically in concert halls all over the world, and even courageously performed on Saturday Night Live. Andraé taught me more about the wonderful diversity of God's creation than anyone I can remember. It wasn't unusual to be at a concert and see people of multiple races. Everyone wanted to be his friend and he was a friend to people from all over the world. He was an ambassador for Christ to be sure!

Now here's the thing: I don't know your story or what might be causing your blood pressure to rise because of this subject. It's not that I don't understand or that I can't sympathize with you. I can to a degree. So, my experiences will mean nothing to you and how you feel about racism.

But this is what God's Word says regarding the issue of the day. This won't take long, because I have just this one passage of Scripture to read to you today. It needs little exposition or explanation. This passage settled my mind and makes me try harder to eradicate this sin of racism which hides in the small dark places of my heart and surprises me when it exposes its ugly head. I hope this Scripture helps you, too. Speaking of Jesus, St. Paul writes to the Church at Ephesus (Ephesians 2:14-18):

> 14 For He, Himself is our peace, who has made the two groups one, and has destroyed the barrier, the dividing wall of hostility, 15 by setting aside in his flesh the law with its commands and regulations. His purpose was to create in himself one new humanity out of the two, thus making peace, 16 and in one body to reconcile both of them to God through the cross, by which he put to death their hostility. 17 He came and preached peace to you who were far away and peace to those who were near. 18 For through him we both have access to the Father by one Spirit.

In its original context, this message refers to breaking down the barriers between Jew and Gentile. In Jewish terms, you were either one of them, or you were a "Goyim." They didn't care if you were from one of the 123 countries we now have in the world. You were one or the other, Jewish or Something Else. There were in that day a lot of us Something Else's.

This ethnic division was the point of painful controversy in the early church. But the Apostle Paul's words should be understood as paradigmatic, that is, an example for the way in which God has acted to break down the walls—to overcome all racial and ethnic divisions in order to create a new people who embody "visible" unity in Christ. That new people is the Church!

Consequently, because "God shows no partiality" (Acts 10:34), the followers of Jesus are called to be ministers of reconciliation, ambassadors for Christ in offering to all the world the promise of the healing of any and all divisions (2 Corinthians 5:17–20). As Jesus taught his disciples, we are to be peacemakers (Matthew 5:9), rejecting the way of division and hatred and violence.

The church lives to be the embodiment of this vision, and it can offer hope to a broken and fearful society such as ours today. And insofar as the Church fails to live into this reality, it compromises the truth of the gospel.

My friends in Christ, if Jesus thought so much of the world to put His own life on the line, no, on a cross, that we might be *one* in Him, how much more, we who have received the benefits of that Cross, that is, forgiveness, life and salvation, should fight with everything in us, to be reconciled with each other.

This sermon wouldn't be complete unless we ask the question, "How will we do this?" I believe if we are willing to listen, God the Spirit will show us how. I know, because the Holy Spirit has used many events in my life to show me.

One last quick story: we have great neighbors who happen to be people of color. From the first day we introduced ourselves to them they became our friends. They are both highly educated, intelligent, and very faithful Christians.

One day we were throwing Frisbees in the back yard and one got over the fence and into their yard. I was about to head over to ask them if we had permission to go back there and get it. But before I got there, it came flying back over the fence.

An hour later I saw them in the front yard and I thanked them for sending the Frisbee back to us. I told them I was sorry the Frisbee ended up in their back yard and that I about to head over to ask them if it was okay to pick it up. And my neighbor said, "Of course, we love you!" I was stunned! And she meant it. I awkwardly garbled a thank you and returned home.

I don't really know anything about their past, good or bad, what kinds of racial indignities they had to endure through life. But this I do know ... Christ is their Lord and because I confessed Christ, I was more to them than just a neighbor. I was their brother in Christ. By His Cross we were reconciled.

Those of us who have not experienced racial animosity may never fully understand the pain that is being expressed today. We don't know how a garage door rope tied in the shape of a noose, an action presumed and ultimately proven innocent by the FBI, and not an act of racism, can evoke fear and anger in a person of color.[1] We can shrug it off as a mistaken conclusion and overreaction, but if you're honest, we all have triggers that bring responses that may seem strange to those who have not lived in our place.

[1]This sermon was delivered the week after a noose was discovered in a NASCAR garage which was the assigned space for the only Black driver in an upcoming race. After an FBI investigation, it was determined that the noose had been tied months before the race and it was impossible to know just who tied it or what their intentions were. Even at the writing of this sermon I questioned the "innocence" of the act. In discussion with the author and an editor of this book, Glen Aubrey, I felt that a footnote was in order to express my discomfort with my description of the FBI findings. Further expansion of this footnote came about after a conversation with another contributor to this book, James Patton. He told me that determining the garage assignments for a future race wasn't that difficult. Those assignments are based on points which the drivers earn and accumulate throughout the season based on their placement at the end of each race. The point spread of the top five drivers are so close that their placement can change with each race. But when you get to the 15th place or lower, the point spreads are so far apart, those garage placements are pretty much set and easy to determine. The point I was trying to make and could have stated more strongly is that the noose is an ugly, historical, and contemporary symbol of racial animosity toward Black populations so that even its appearance in a race track garage evokes strong emotions. The NASCAR organization should be applauded for making such a strong and unified show of support of their "brother" driver and for their condemnation and intolerance of racism in their organization.

Scripture says," If it is possible, as far as it depends on you, live at peace with everyone." I pray that we, the church, may learn to show sympathy and understanding to those who are so full of rage because of the injustices shown to so many people of color in our time. We don't have to condone unlawful acts of violence and rioting, but we do need to show God's love and acceptance for every child of God.

Law and Order is the way of worldly governance. But we are called to a higher law, the Law of Love.

May God give us His Holy Spirit so that we may become Reconcilers and Ambassadors of Jesus, and through Him show the world a better way to bring peace to our hostile world. Amen.

Law and Order is the way of worldly governance.
But we are called to a higher law, the Law of Love.

Pastor Vernon Lintvedt: "Racism"

*****

Author's Note: **Vernon Lintvedt** is a friend from High School. He is one of my dearest friends. We have known each other for 50+ years. He is a gifted leader and has pastored his church in O'Fallon, Illinois for well over 20 years. Vernon is humble, fun-loving, sincere, dedicated, a truth-teller, an accurate expositor of Scripture, and gifted singer as well. See ***Faith Matters***, www.FaithMattersToYou.com for a reference to the vocal group of which we both were a part in the 1970s, ***Light of Love***. In June, 2020, I was attending church 'online' when I heard the sermon you just read. Vernon and his church are, in a word, "authentic." If his footnote to the NASCAR event entry proves anything, it's that Vern is authentic to the core. Connecting with my dear friend, James Patton, in preparation for the finalization of the book, dealing with the malady of racism and its eradication was the right action to take, one believer to another. What Vernon did not say, but James Patton does say in his chapter (Chapter 10, "Who Is My Neighbor"), is that James is Black. Vernon, James, and I are truly brothers in Christ, regardless of race. We love each other. Our collective desires are to be "Reconcilers and Ambassadors of Jesus, and through Him show the world a better way to bring peace to our hostile world."

Chapter 3
Grief Has No Expiration Date

Terry Burgess
Author *When Our Blue Star Turned Gold*

Dedicated to Army Air Corps Veteran and Former POW Fiske Hanley

August 3, 2020

I would have sacrificed anything to have my comfortable, humdrum life back.

I know that sounds a bit ironic, but before tragedy struck, I had no idea of what a sheltered, peaceful, and idyllic life I had been leading. Like most people, my wife and I got up early every weekday morning, stumbled through our morning routine, took the train to our offices, worked our eight hours, travelled home, ate supper, watched a TV show, played with our cats, visited social media sites, and then went quietly to bed to doze until the alarm went off starting the boring, yet comfortable, cycle all over.

Then one normal, routine morning in March of 2011 our telephone rang, and with just a few words our idyllic, peaceful, boring, comfortable, and clueless life was completely shattered.

When I try to put those few, yet horrid words to paper, they just do not convey the sheer impact they had on us. My daughter-in-law, Tiffany, told us through her tearful sobs and gasps for air that our son, Bryan, had been killed in action in Afghanistan very early that morning. Her husband, her children's father, my son, was gone.

My world—our world—was forever changed.

In the hours, days, and weeks that followed, the routine, day-to-day activities that we had taken for granted simply no longer mattered. Every aspect of our life, from personal hygiene, to eating, to sleeping, to working, had changed perspective: from seemingly crucial to being unessential. They simply just no longer mattered. I lost my job because I seemed to be un-focused, combative, and mentally absent. I began taking too many pills and too many drinks and sleeping most of the day. I lost interest in almost everything, becoming so withdrawn that my wife felt like she had lost me along with my son.

Family, friends, and neighbors who had been so supportive during the first few months following Bryan's death began to back away from us because of my inability to respond coherently to any show of sympathy. I was angry that the world had not stopped turning. I was frustrated that I had no earthly way to avenge Bryan's death. I was exasperated that I could not hold accountable those who were responsible for his death.

To my mind, there wasn't a thing on earth or in heaven that could fix my broken heart. I was in hell and I wanted the world to burn with me. My traumatized brain convinced me that if Bryan could not be brought back to life then there was no reason for life to continue.

But life did.

"You never know how strong you are until being strong is the only choice you have." ~Bob Marley

Weeks later, I was sitting in my wooden chair on the back deck, absently scratching and digging into the arm of the chair with a loose nail I had found, when my vision very suddenly cleared and I focused on the letters I had just carved into the wood: **Bryan**

Like a slap to the face I realized I was doing nothing to honor my son. I was doing absolutely nothing to live up to his sacrifice. As long as I did nothing, Bryan's death would be in vain.

I was raised in a Christian family in a small, west Texas town where people waved at each other from front porches and vehicles. Where the checkers at the grocery store knew the price of every item and knew you and your mama by name. Friday night football was the highlight of the week and a monthly trip to Abilene for supplies gave us a chance to spend our hard-earned allowance on a special toy or a record album. The Fourth of July was anticipated and celebrated, yet I only remember us observing Memorial Day as simply a three-day weekend. (I had never before heard the term 'Gold Star' used outside of grade school or Sunday school, and my family never spoke of their time in the armed forces.)

Death came only in the form of an announcement in church on Sunday morning or by a telephone call on the party line. Death was not frequent but it was completely normal for elderly people to pass away. We polished our best shoes, got dressed in black, and carried a casserole to the home of the family of the deceased.

Other times, a pet dog got run over by a pickup truck being driven too fast; a pet cat got into a fight with a rattlesnake—and lost. We'd bury them out near the barn, shed a few tears, and then inevitably a different dog or kitten would show up at the farm and all would be right with the world.

Death was never near and he never lingered.

You are never given a handbook or instruction manual on how to handle death. Who in their right mind would willingly attend a grief seminar when we are taught from early-on that death is natural and to be expected? My grandparents passed away, one at a time over several years; uncles and aunts passed away and we attended their funerals, shed the tears, ate the casseroles, accepted the condolences, and then went home. The time for grieving was over.

I thought I had dealt with death. Yes, Bryan was serving in the U.S. Army. He was overseas fighting the Global War on Terrorism. He was fifteen days away from coming home. Any thought of him being killed was squashed in the back of my mind under hundreds of happy plans for his homecoming party and his upcoming 30th birthday. Such a tragedy could never befall us. Such things just didn't happen to our family. God would never allow that to happen to us.

One bullet. One phone call. My faith died with my son.

My uncle Bobby on my mother's side passed away the day we buried Bryan. Mom was very sick with Parkinson's and a broken hip so she couldn't attend her brother's funeral. I had just returned home from Bryan's funeral at Fort Campbell, Kentucky and my brother, Lynn, and I loaded up and headed to Oklahoma. Uncle Bob had served in the U.S. Army. He was given a military funeral. I had to walk away from the ceremony when the Army Corps started folding the flag to Taps being played in the background. I later apologized to the family and to their credit they understood my behavior.

Mom passed away the following December. My wife's dad passed away the next January. Her mom passed away less than a year later and our cat had to be put to sleep the day before her mom's funeral. My cousin, who was my age, passed away the next year.

It felt like Death had moved in with us.

During all of this I was still being haunted by the fact that I was doing nothing to honor Bryan. Beth was terrified that she would come home some afternoon only to find that I had lost my battle with grief. I wasn't sleeping much at night and even when I did sleep, I struggled with terrifying nightmares. She was afraid to leave me alone.

She began searching online for organizations that helped Gold Star families—those who had lost a loved one in service to our country. She found many organizations that were founded to support Gold Star moms and Gold Star wives and Gold Star families, but nothing that specifically recognized Gold Star dads. At Bryan's funeral I had met the fathers of the five other soldiers who had been killed in the same battle as Bryan. I knew I was not alone in my grief; that they were mourning the loss of their sons, also.

At the funerals at Fort Campbell, an organization, The Patriot Guard Riders (PGR), astride dozens of motorcycles, escorted the families to the funeral homes. It was an incredible display of honor and patriotism. Tiffany, Bryan's wife, told me he had left his 2005 Yamaha V-Star motorcycle to me. A glimmer of hope sparked in me and I not only learned to ride the bike but I also joined our local Patriot Guard Riders group and began attending missions at Dallas-Fort Worth National Cemetery. They recognized me as a Gold Star dad and even asked me to perform a eulogy for a veteran who had no living family members. I felt as though my grief was being recognized and that I was coming full circle in honoring Bryan.

After hearing my story of struggling with grief and trying to find ways to honor Bryan, a fellow PGR member suggested organizing a type of retreat for Gold Star parents, to bring us together and create a network of support. The idea took root and Beth and I started contacting other Gold Star parents in Texas and we discovered a discouraging lack of support for the moms and dads of fallen soldiers. We found a nice, scenic, and secluded town in south Texas with facilities to accommodate thirty families, and we conducted our first Gold Star Parent's Retreat. The Retreat was a sold-out event with parents from all across Texas attending. We learned from the other moms and dads that they, too, had been searching for some way to deal with their grief and find some way to honor their sons and daughters.

The success of the first retreat spurred us to become a registered non-profit organization, and we had conducted annual, sold-out retreats up until the 2020 COVID-19 disaster forced us to cancel the event for that year. We stayed in touch with our Gold Star parents via social media, but *nothing can replace the feel of a heart-felt hug or the sound of laughter from someone who truly thought they would never laugh again.*

The phrase "The New Normal" had been bandied about during the outbreak and quarantine by some of those who had never had to deal with a true tragedy. Gold Star parents have been living "The New Normal" since that horrible phone call or knock on the door told them their son or daughter was not coming home.

Statistics failed to give a true story of the 2020 outbreak. Statistics for Gold Star moms and dads have failed to prevent job loss, divorces, and sadly, suicides. It takes an action to invoke a reaction. *Doing nothing equals getting nothing done.* Yes, there are things in this world that will push us to our limits. What you do when you reach that limit is up to you alone. You can let grief consume you or you can ask for help. Trust me: you're stronger than you think. If you believe in God and Jesus and the Saints, let that be your rock. If you believe in your spouse, do so with all of your heart, mind, and soul, but you must first believe in yourself.

Bryan was with his squad on that mountainside in Afghanistan when that bullet tore through him. One other of his squad was shot and killed while trying to cover Bryan and get him to safety. Yet another member of the squad was shot, not fatally, while he covered both of his teammates. Bryan was coherent enough to apologize for dying. He felt like he had let them down. One of them told me later that he would have followed Bryan through Hell itself if necessary. I assured him that he had.

You may have felt like you had been going through hell on earth during the 2020 pandemic. I know I felt that way. Some people have never faced an adverse situation which can cause so much controversy; especially one that can divide a nation between those that felt they must wear a protective mask constantly and those who thought we are being socially controlled.

Family, friends, and neighbors became divided on what to do, when, about what. But as the saying goes, "This, too, shall pass." As we've all seen, actions during the meantime can affect the difference between peace and conflict. You don't have to choose between being a 'sheep' or a terrorist during adverse times. Just be yourself. Many people seem to have forgotten the Golden Rule of Matthew 7:12: "Do unto others as you would have them do unto you."

When Beth and I could not find the resources or help we needed to recover from our son's death, we started our own resource and wound up helping many others in the process. It's not an easy thing to do, and when we hear from people in other states that they have no resources to turn to, our advice to them is, "Start your own program." Find friends and seek out people with similar needs; create a simple support group; use social media to connect; share your thoughts, feelings, and fears, and you'll be surprised at the support (and empathy) you receive in return.

As human beings capable of free thought we resist being told what to do. We live in a great nation where free thought and freedom of speech are encouraged. Even though those rights are, at times, taken to extremes, we are all free to express ourselves. My family endured many different opinions about the Global War on Terrorism after Bryan was killed. Our resolve to honor his sacrifice and share his story kept us strong and made us adaptable to adversity.

Resilience is a word we use a lot. People constantly tell us they are amazed at how strong we are and how proud they are of us for overcoming our grief. Those who have survived traumatic experiences and have managed to come out the other side appearing to all the rest of the world to be a normal, whole, and sound of mind person are my heroes. I can see the invisible masks they wear in public. The public does not see the weak-kneed, puking-in-the-toilet, wall-punching fits that haunt us when we're alone.

At times, even family will fail those who have deep-seated grief. My dad told me that I was too obsessed with Bryan's death, that I had grieved enough, and that I needed to put my grieving behind me and do something positive with my life. That was after we had successfully started our Gold Star Parents Retreat. I wanted to lash out back at him, to yell at him that my grief still felt raw, but I literally bit my tongue, I left his house and didn't talk to him for almost two years after that.

Glen Aubrey of Creative Team Publishing, the author, editor (compiler), and publisher of ***God's Plan Unfolding * Strength and Renewal in Times of Crisis,*** had encouraged me to put our story in writing and he published my book, ***When Our Blue Star Turned Gold***.

One of my brothers gave our dad a copy of the book and to my total surprise dad called me out of the blue and asked if he could have a dozen more copies to give to his friends. I didn't need to hash anything else out with dad, and we again visit regularly.

I discovered that so many things we take for granted are tenuous at best. Many people had discovered that, too, during the pandemic, love, faith, hope; they can all be gone in an instant. The wonderful thing is that they can also be created in an instant. This world today is not forever. We are not forever, but our actions—good or bad—just may be.

The fact that you are reading this indicates that you are one of those rare individuals who are willing to look at both sides before making your own judgement. I have no way of knowing what you have experienced or are currently going through, but now you know that there is probably someone who does.

Any one of us can affect a positive change.

I discovered that so many things we take for granted are tenuous at best. Many people have discovered that, too, during this current pandemic. Love, faith, hope; they can all be gone in an instant. The wonderful thing is that they can also be created in an instant.

This world today is not forever. We are not forever, but our actions—good or bad—just may be. The fact that you are reading this indicates that you are one of those rare individuals who are willing to look at both sides before making your own judgement.

We know many Gold Stars who have secluded themselves almost to the point of denying their child was killed. They do not wish to attend events because it is 'too hard' to be reminded of the tragedy.

Beth and I chose a different path. We freely shared Bryan's story. We shared our pain and in doing so gained many acquaintances that we would have never met otherwise, much less befriended, because of Bryan. His name and his story are now known coast-to-coast because we took ourselves out of our comfort zone of self-pity and put ourselves back into the world.

It is a world much changed for us, but we have many friends who are amazing patriots and many of them are warriors who very nearly lost their own lives. We've met celebrities including Medal of Honor recipients, movie stars, country and western superstars, sports legends, and powerful politicians. We've been on several radio and T.V. shows. Our home is so filled with memorabilia of events held in Bryan's honor that one visitor called the entire house a 'shrine.' We would trade it all to have Bryan physically with us. I take comfort in knowing that he is spiritually with us.

While our Retreats seem to take on a very spiritual feel, the Retreats themselves are not 'faith-based' and we do not lecture our guests on how to 'move on' from their grief.

Grieving does not have an expiration date.

We simply welcome any parent of any fallen son or daughter who raised their right hand and took an oath to defend our country; regardless of branch of service or cause of death. We open our doors to those parents who have become jobless, divorced, and even unwelcome at other organizations. We know the pain of losing a child.

Even though Bryan was an adult and a warrior, he was still my son. I cannot imagine the pain of losing a child to suicide, or murder, or illness, or an accident, and then having an organization that is supposed to support survivors turn you away because your child was not killed in combat.

As odd as it seems to me at times, I am now comfortable with Bryan's death. The nightmares have ceased; I no longer have any thoughts of self-harm; and we look forward to spending time with the other Gold Star parents we have met along the way. That is not to say that I wouldn't still trade the past few years to have Bryan back with us; I have simply come to terms with his death. I know without a doubt that the human spirit lives on. I will 'see' Bryan again, and I truly hope that our spirits have the ability to hug without the need for social distancing.

*****

Author's Note: **Terry Burgess'** book, ***When Our Blue Star Turned Gold*** is one of the most moving accounts of military service and sacrifice we have ever had the opportunity to publish at Creative Team Publishing. His story will inspire you, as it has thousands of other readers. His book and the story behind Gold Star Retreats were featured live on NBC's *Today Show*.
Please access the book by going to this website: https://goldstarparent.com/. Be uplifted, challenged, encouraged, and hope-filled.

Chapter 4
At Issue Is Our Schools

Richard A. Redd, MD

September 8, 2020

The importance of our schools and the teachers who impart daily understanding and wisdom to our children in the United States of America is incalculable. Proper education is the life-blood of our country and our world. I thank God for the school system we have, though it is far from perfect. Sometimes it takes a crisis, where we have a critical part of our culture taken away, before we realize how vital that part is and how much we have taken it for granted. We naively believe that our system of schools will *always* be here, but it only takes a local or nation-wide tragedy to prove that it can be removed abruptly in a day, with all the dire consequences associated with that circumstance.

If we are wise, and if we are looking and listening for God's guidance, we will see that all catastrophic events are designed to teach us significant and important lessons. They show us where we are strong, but also where our defenses need to be shored up.

The COVID-19 pandemic of 2020 was no exception. With the data we had on hand (which was usually less than what we would have liked or needed), we limited the damage to our country from outside sources and then launched an all-out effort to defeat the virus at home. No campaign like this was perfect; there are too many unknown variables. Ours was a noble effort and generally well-executed.

The devastation that the virus wreaked was significant. As it waned, we saw its effect on the American landscape. Many Americans died, contributing to a tragedy of monumental proportions. That is potential we shall never recoup. The economic toll is still being calculated but is in the billions of dollars lost. Countless people lost businesses and jobs, and the political climate became more rancorous and divisive than at any time in recent recorded history.

Sociologically, people were isolated from each other and especially loved ones. Schools and churches were closed as it was feared that the disease would spread with dire consequences if social distancing was not maintained. This limited much of the spiritual healing and comfort we would have otherwise obtained, as well as retarding education of our children.

As is usually the case, many positive results were also evident. Many people became more dependent on and thankful to God for their safety and livelihood. I believe that we developed a greater respect for our fellow citizens as we looked out for the health and welfare of each other. We became less dependent on other nations for critical equipment and supplies (antibiotics from China, for example). I think most people realized the importance of having some extra cash, food, and supplies available even if they didn't live in a hurricane, earthquake, or tornado-prone area of the country. People also learned the importance of good hygiene in the prevention of the spread of disease. Many developed the habit of washing their hands and cleaning contaminated surfaces and equipment regularly.

As the country began to open up, the safety of all American citizens became a concern as we began to congregate and enjoy each other's company again. This was especially true as thoughts moved to reopening our schools.

Depending on the crisis, children will either be at increased risk for illness or injury, or not. The COVID-19 virus spared most children, and it was thought that they were not a common vector for spreading the disease. Influenza and the cold virus, on the other hand, have affected children in previous winter seasons, and it is rapidly spread from child to child and from child to adult. The crisis should, therefore, determine the response we take and the policies we set.

There is no doubt and little debate on whether the schools should reopen. They are an essential service to our nation. What might be done to enhance the safety of the children, teachers, and school administrators as we reopen? Clearly as schools do reopen these recommendations should continue to be employed:

1. Pray for guidance, asking God to supervise the process as it unfolds.
2. Pray for wisdom for our political leaders and those in charge of the administration of our schools.
3. Pray for teachers that they will impart a positive attitude to their students.
4. Pray for students who will be naturally be anxious, especially at the first of the school year and beyond.
5. Screen children and adults before entering the school each day with an infrared No Touch forehead thermometer ($50). Anyone with a fever greater than 100.4° F should be sent home or urged to go directly to a medical facility for evaluation. Screening should capture many forms of communicable disease, such as influenza, pneumonia, and ear infections, all of which may start with fever. Screening will *not* capture everyone, though, so we should continue to monitor the health and welfare of students and teachers during the school day and disposition accordingly.
6. Control access to the school building by unlocking only one or two doors in the morning. This will limit the number of screeners needed and limit the number of unscreened people getting into the building.
7. Document who is screened by name at the start of each school day. Keep a checklist, and keep these lists

securely filed away should you need them again in the future.

8. Ask teachers to send any students who are not feeling well to an isolated area in the school where their temperatures can be measured and they can be held until the parents can pick up their child.
9. If face coverings are mandated by governmental authorities, teachers should wear clear plastic face shields in the school so that children can see their facial expressions while teaching. This may allay fear in the younger children.
10. Students, teachers, administrative staff, and parents should be taught methods of healthy living in order to bolster their immune systems, and then be encouraged to practice these methods. This is likely the best way to protect yourself and your loved ones from any virus or infectious outbreak, which is sure to come our way in the future. These methods may include, but are not limited to:
    a. Eating a healthy, balanced diet, including low-carbohydrates, moderate protein, and healthy fats
    b. Maintaining adequate hydration
    c. Safe supplements. Consult with knowledgeable individuals as to dose and frequency of the following:
        - Vitamin D3
        - Vitamin C
        - Betaglucan
        - Astragulus

- Vitamin E
- Magnesium
- Zinc

d. Moderate daily exercise

e. Minimum of 8 hours of uninterrupted sleep per night for adults; children usually require a minimum of 10 hours.

f. Maintain a positive attitude no matter what your situation or the circumstances you find yourself in. There is no benefit to a negative attitude, and no excuse not to have a positive attitude, especially if we are Christian believers.

g. Educate yourself on the facts to the best of your ability and search for the truth to allay fear.

h. Build your faith.

i. Pray and/or meditate to decrease stress.

j. Help and encourage others. You may be surprised how good it makes you feel.

11. Aerosolized droplets containing viruses will stay suspended in the air a shorter period of time when the humidity in the classroom is slightly increased.
12. It is better to be outside when possible, rather than inside.
13. Open windows slightly to create a cross-draft.
14. Maintain proper distancing (6 feet).
15. Encourage coughing or sneezing into your own elbow to confine the area of contamination as much as possible.

16. Have hand sanitizers (minimum of 60% alcohol) available for use in all classrooms and offices.
17. Require appropriate hand-washing before and after meals, after going to the bathroom, after touching contaminated equipment, or after touch one's face. Touching another person's face is obviously unwise.
18. Minimize group size, as required or urged by state or local officials.
19. Get buy-in from as many people at your school as possible for the policies you believe are reasonable. Listen to any concerns and research all points of view. Analyze these views against the facts that you know are true. Those who object may be correct, and all would benefit from their opinion/expertise if they are correct.

Further information on building personal immunity can be obtained from my book, ***All-In or Nothing***. It is available at my website, **www.all-inornothing.com**, or from Amazon or Barnes & Noble.

*****

Preparation for possible future crises is key. When they occur, the impact can be less disturbing.

In his book, *Resilient Warriors,* Bob Dees eloquently discusses the necessity of being prepared for setback or calamity ahead of time, so that we can weather the storms of life more effectively (with God's help), and emerge stronger and more capable on the other side. [1]

[1] Dees, Robert F. *Resilient Warriors*. San Diego: Creative Team Publishing, 2011, pages 67-75. See Resources at the conclusion of this book.

Some policies, like wearing masks during the COVID 19 pandemic, may be difficult to accept, and others will occur in the future. Keep the best interest of those at greatest risk in mind. Gather facts to support your position, and be willing to share those facts with others.

If we are confronted with other respiratory viruses down the road, here are a few things to remember about N95 respirators, bandanas, or cloth masks. There have been no randomized controlled clinical trials (the gold-standard of medical research) which have proven that masks will prevent viral spread. In seventeen of the best studies in the medical literature on influenza, no conclusive relationship between mask/respirator use and protection against influenza could be found. Assuming that viruses are approximately equal in size (0.1-0.2 microns), we can deduce that the results would be the same for other viruses.

Are there dangers or side-effects when the wearing masks, especially for prolonged periods of time (more than two hours at a time)? Yes, there are. These include headaches, dizziness, decreased oxygen levels in the blood (reduced from 98% to 90% within two minutes), increased carbon dioxide levels in the blood, increased airway resistance, and rebreathing viruses and bacteria which are already in the nasal passages. The benefits of wearing a mask should outweigh the risks before you acquiesce. Wearing a mask may be especially problematic for older individuals; consider substituting a face shield for the mask.

All that being said: you may still *choose* to comply with policies that you don't completely agree with. Some states may levy large fines ($500-5000) for not complying. Also keep in mind that the goal of opening schools is to better educate our children (and for some it also means that both parents can go back to work). In consideration of a private school or home school, you would want to do everything possible to keep the doors open.

Assuming that schools will reopen after a catastrophic event, what kind of an educational system are we sending our kids back to? Our educational system is one of the most expensive in the world. In 2017, the United States of America spent as average of $12,201 per pupil per year on education. That is an average of $158,613 per pupil for a K-12 education. State educational budgets vary with population (New York $70 million, Texas $63 million, Oregon $7.9 million and Wyoming $1.9 million). The cost per pupil was highest in New York ($23,000 per pupil per year).

We want our schools to be graduating the best people and the best citizens we can possibly produce. We want thousands of excited and motivated high school graduates to go on to college and excel at their chosen vocations. We need their expertise as a nation; each child has unique talents to give.

Any catastrophic event can fundamentally change the way students are taught, especially as we get better and better with remote learning. This may be one of the major reasons that technology (bandwidth and laptops) has moved into the remote areas of the country and into the larger, more densely populated cities.

It is logical to assume, since we are spending an exorbitant amount of money educating our children, that our children ought to rank very high in the world in academics (international tests). In fact, they do not. In 2013, the most recent scores I could find, among 34 Organization for Economic Cooperation and Development (OECD) nations, United States 15-year old students ranked 26th in math, 17th in reading and 21st in science. Only 9% of American students were "top performers". One in four (25%) of U.S. students did not reach level two of mathematics proficiency (where they have incorporated skills that will enable them to participate effectively and productively in life and society). Only 7% of students were classified as resilient, meaning they performed much better than predicted based on their socio-economic class.

Since we spend so much for our children's education, where is the return on our investment? I no longer have children in school, but I still pay a hefty amount every year in property taxes, of which school taxes are a part. I want our kids to be the best they can be, and I want our schools to be well-supplied.

Our current system is failing our children and is setting them up to fail on the international stage. We surely can and must do better than this. If you educate your children at home, there are moves afoot to divert funds from public schools to parents, as vouchers. This could also happen if you choose to move your children to private school (secular or religious).

87% of students in the United States of American attend public school, with 10% in private schools and 3% in home schools. More parents may see the wisdom in choosing to put their children in private school or home-school, especially if the costs go down with vouchers.

So, in the interest of reopening, but also improving our schools, I would like to propose that we not only send our kids back to school as soon as we can, and keep schools open, but that we also take this time to upgrade the American education system in order to more effectively educate our children. The one-size-fits-all model which is currently in place is not working. Public school has become an expensive forum which has little association with meaningful education. It is also becoming unhinged from the Judeo-Christian ethic, the Constitutional republican form of government and the capitalistic economic system upon which our country is based, and by which our country has succeeded more than any other country over the years. Restoring our educational system to its rightful position of prominence in this country and returning to our historical, societal roots is paramount to elevating the United States of America to its rightful position of power and influence in the world again. We need to be that "shining city on the hill," which serves as a beacon of excellence throughout the world, and to which other countries can aspire.

How do we improve the American school system? First, we keep the structure or organization which is currently in place, i.e. public, private, or home school. We give parents a choice about where they want their children to go to school, and subsidize their choice with vouchers. After gaining a fundamental education in primary (grades 1-6), middle (grades 7-8) and high school (grades 9-12), students have the option of going to the university or college of their choice, military service (through which they can continue their education), junior college/vocational school, or directly into the work force. Those who do not attend college or university right away can spin back into tertiary education through the back door by attending college, on-line college or adult education courses when they are sure of what they want to do.

A meaningful difference in the way children are taught must occur at the K-12 level. We need to take a more personal interest in the students, helping them to understand themselves and their strengths. Knowing their temperaments and intelligences would add a lot, and move us away from the one-size-fits-all philosophy of education, which is anything but personal.

Education is cumulative, and students need to be encouraged to excel by continuing to practice reading, writing, speaking eloquently, and applying mathematics in their daily lives. I would suggest year-round education to prevent the significant information "dump" which occurs over the summer months. This will create a solid foundation for success in later years.

Grade levels are appropriately stratified by age presently. Within each classroom, we find twenty-five to thirty students on average, and one teacher. There is usually no teacher's aide. The student's competency ranges from high to low. One teacher addresses all levels of student expertise. This system of education is not fair or effective for anyone, teacher or students. Teachers are frustrated. The bright students are bored, and the academically challenged students are overwhelmed. No one learns optimally.

Why not divide each grade level vertically as well, according to the student's competency? For example, if there are 100 children in second grade at Lincoln Elementary School, divide the students into 5 groups/sections of 20 students each or 10 groups of 10 students each. Each section would have its own teacher. A smaller student/teacher ratio is ideal because students will learn better when they can interact frequently and directly with their teacher/mentor.

At the beginning of the school year, students would be placed in a section based on their performance in the previous year. If a student is new to the school, he or she can be initially placed in a middle section or take a placement test to determine their appropriate section. Students are evaluated or graded each day, and after six weeks, the students are moved into new sections based on how they have performed. Those who score well move up to a higher section; those who are having trouble, move down. As a result, students are matched with other students who are roughly at the same academic level. Teachers can teach to the level of the students; teachers also have the luxury of spending more time in areas where the students need it. Everybody wins. Students learn, teachers teach effectively.

What about self-esteem? Isn't it crushed if students move down? Not at all. Some students are strong in math and science, others in literature and foreign languages. Vertical stratification allows students to find their strengths naturally. They are happier and less stressed.

This system is used at the United States service academies at West Point and Annapolis. It is known as the Thayer System, and was developed at West Point by Sylvanus Thayer in the early 1800s. It works. West Point engineers usually come from the upper sections, armor and artillery officers from the upper and middle sections, and infantry officers from the lower sections. Parenthetically, officers who reach the rank of Brigadier General or above have come from any/all of the sections. All graduates are well prepared to succeed.

Finally, we should make it a national priority to ensure that there are good computers in every school and for every student, and there is sufficient bandwidth to insure excellent speed and service.

By the way, the question may arise as to whether the students should be passed up to the next grade if the school year is significantly shortened. That depends on the student and the parents of each child.

Athletes should have full eligibility to play their sport.

The students have had no part in causing a national catastrophe and should not be penalized for it. Whatever is best for the student should serve as the standard by which we make these decisions.

As a general rule, a solid education sets the foundation for a successful life. We owe our children nothing less.

*****

Chapter 5
Death and Grief

Angela Williams
Contracting Officer
United States Federal Government
Author *Knowing You Have Done Your Best * No Regrets*

August 6, 2020

One can say I have had my fair share, or more than my fair share of Death and Grief. We are all logical and know that death comes to all of us at some time. This doesn't make it any easier, however. I can say this: were it not for the love of God and His constant blessings I receive every day, I am not sure how I would make it through this day.

You may be going through struggles and think that no one understands or could ever comprehend what is happening. I cannot say enough that *you are not alone,* and never will be alone even when you feel the world is crashing all around you.

God's love is all around us, even though we may think it's hard to see with all the chaos going on. I find it helps to take a few minutes to just sit and quiet the mind. You will start to hear and feel that love. It may take a little while, but you will start to hear a faint sound, or recall a memory that makes you smile, or remember a song that lets you know He is there with you. For me it's always been a smell – like my mom's cooking, and birds. I have a pair of doves that follow me no matter where I am. I always smile because I know this is God's way of showing me He is always with me.

The God of All Comfort: In 2 Corinthians 1:3, 4: [3] Praise be to the God and Father of our Lord Jesus Christ, the Father of compassion and the God of all comfort, [4] who comforts us in all our troubles, so that we can comfort those in any trouble with the comfort we ourselves have received from God.

Even as I am writing this on this day with all that is occurring, not only in my life's work, but in crises which so many have to deal with, in that world I am finding peace. I am tearful, but in a very good way. It is like a burden is being lifted even if it's just a small one, but lifting the small burden enough to give me the strength I need to get focused and power through what is either upsetting me or blocking my way to get my job done.

I understand how hard it is to have faith. To this day I struggle. Maybe the reason is this: maybe we feel we must be in control of everything in our lives. Personally, I am still learning how to let go of some of that control, and just have faith.

I was encouraged to write a book and I found out just how much it helped me with some lingering issues, lingering issues I had thought I dealt with. That book is ***Knowing You Have Done Your Best * No Regrets.*** It can be obtained: www.knowingyouhavedoneyourbest.com

I want to encourage all of you to start a personal journal, or find a quiet place where you can enjoy a few minutes just for yourself.

From 1 Corinthians 1:3: Grace and peace to you from God our Father and the Lord Jesus Christ.

*****

Author's Note: **Angela Williams** is a true friend. We originally met in Gettysburg, Pennsylvania. She is a truth-teller, unashamedly so. As her book, ***Knowing You Have Done Your Best * No Regrets*** graphically demonstrates, she possesses a caring, vulnerable, and loving heart. She offers creative, effective solutions to many of our societal issues, including feeding the homeless and meeting the needs of veterans. At Creative Team Publishing, we are grateful for the opportunity to publish her. Her story will motivate you, as it has many, including national TV audiences.

Chapter 6
The COVID-19 Pandemic

Hiren Raval
Registered Pharmacist
Haslet, Texas

August 6, 2020

I am Hiren Raval, a registered pharmacist. I would like to share my experiences and opinions on the COVID-19 pandemic of 2020.

As a healthcare professional, I served many patients with COVID-19. After recovery, many patients have come to me with interesting feedback about their experience. I would like to elaborate on three client's/patient's feedback, received in June and July, 2020.

The first case was regarding a family of four people (parents and two kids) who became infected. The father recovered fast once he was quarantined for two weeks along with taking his medications. The two kids also recovered easily from COVID-19. Unfortunately, the mother (his wife) stayed in the hospital for around thirty days and was yet to recover by the time of this writing. Due to the hospital policy, the rest of the family was restricted from meeting her.

I came to know of their situation as the father came to pick up medications one day. He told me of his experience, and thanked God. A month before his family's situation he had received a layoff. Fortunately, he immediately applied for private insurance and was able to support his family's needs. He felt blessed after this incident.

The second case was of one worker in a factory who manufactured seats for airplanes. Due to the COVID-19 pandemic, all flights had been cancelled and all airlines were not placing any orders to upgrade their aircraft seats. His company started cutting hours, and to maintain social distancing, workers had to work alternating weeks. During his week off, he went to a local lake for fishing. He and his family became conservative in spending on their healthcare needs for fear of no work.

The last case I talk about was of a senior citizen. Although he was infected, he did not have any complications. He found out when he had COVID-19 when he went to the hospital because he was not feeling well. Once the hospital staff tested him, he was told he was COVID-19 positive. They checked him for other conditions and then told him to go home and quarantine for two weeks with prescription medications. Three weeks later he arrived at my pharmacy and told me about the incident and that he had recovered easily.

As a pharmacist working every day, I had definitely noticed changes in my patients' shopping behaviors. Most customers had come to the drive-thru window to drop off and pick up their prescriptions. Those who didn't drop off and pick up their medications preferred delivery at their home. I had also noticed that the purchases of immunity booster supplements and vitamins were increasing.

To support and aid the community, I am developing a dietary supplement product to boost the natural immunity of the body and prepare the body to fight any bacterial or viral infections. The product will be a combination of vitamins and herbal extracts of various edible herbs.

The key to surviving in the COVID-19 pandemic was to keep your body healthy and build your body's natural immunity in order to be able to handle any kind of bacterial or viral outbreaks.

And as a result of the COVID-19 outbreak, my family and I became very conscious about what we are eating and drinking. We considered lifestyle changes: we thought about starting to farm and grow our own foods, and engaging in Yoga and meditation.

I am encouraging my children to join the healthcare field after they graduate from high school. That vocation provides knowledge on taking good care of their health, along with providing healthcare services to help other people. Plus, we are becoming passionate about taking care of Mother Nature by reducing pollution and protecting natural habitats. We are becoming convinced that getting closer to nature and changing our lifestyles can help to avoid this kind of pandemic in future.

May God bless us all.

*****

Author's Note: **Hiren Raval** is a kind and caring pharmacist, a dedicated professional who is courteous, takes time for his customers; he is truly interested in the welfare of those he serves. He is a healthcare professional who is a blessing in so many ways. He is an encourager. He has a contagious laugh and pleasant demeanor. It is a true pleasure to see him represented in this book, ***God's Plan Unfolding * Strength and Renewal in Times of Crisis.*** Thank you, Hiren, for your stories and perspectives. Further, I don't know many pharmacists who also actively promote vitamins and herbal extracts of edible herbs to fight bacterial or viral infections. He is one healthcare professional worth knowing!

Chapter 7
Thoughts on the News Media in Today's Crazy, Politically Charged Culture

Barry Willey U.S. Army COL, Retired,
Former Public Affairs Officer (PAO)
Author *Out of the Valley * An Amazing Life Story That Can Help You Make Good Choices... and Leave an Eternal Legacy* and *Extreme Investing * Changing the World One Believer at a Time*

August 7, 2020

Thomas Jefferson, one of our founding fathers (though some now doubt his importance because of his slave-holding past), said something very profound, which most of us never knew he said.

In a letter from Paris in 1787, to a delegate he had sent to the Continental Congress – Edward Carrington – he wrote the following:

> "The people are the only censors of their governors: and even their errors will tend to keep these to the true principles of their institution. To punish these errors too severely would be to suppress the only safeguard of the public liberty. The way to prevent these irregular interpositions of the people is to give them full information of their affairs thro' the channel of the public papers, and to contrive that those papers should penetrate the whole mass of the people. The basis of our governments being the opinion of the people, the very first object should be to keep that right; and were it left to me to decide whether we should have a government without newspapers or newspapers without a government, I should not hesitate a moment to prefer the latter. But I should mean that every man should receive those papers and be capable of reading them."

Why that early in the establishment of our new Nation, would Jefferson comment in such a profoundly odd way—praising the newspapers of that day as a key part of a fledgling country? I'll tell you why! It's the media's job—past media, current media, future media ... all media—to be *very* curious ... and *very* skeptical of anything that anybody says ... whatever party says it! That's why Jefferson said what he did about newspapers and that's why it's so important to let them do their jobs. If they aren't using facts and aren't balanced (except for opinion pieces), then hold them accountable and stop reading and subscribing to their paper ... make it hurt in their pocket books.

Before I go any further, allow me to provide some bona fides. Part of my 29 years as an active duty Army officer, I was a qualified Public Affairs Officer (PAO). Military PAOs work with unit commanders to interface with news media and help tell the Army's great story, while also sharing truthfully when challenging times and negative things occur.

Two thirds of my time in uniform I was an Infantry Officer. The other third, I dealt with news media—papers, magazines, radio, TV ... all of the media available to the public. The Army sent me to one of the most distinguished Journalism Schools in the USA, The Ernie Pyle School of Journalism at Indiana University. I received a Master's degree in Journalism.

I was the media interface with the 82nd Airborne Division during the invasion of Granada in 1983, whose mission was to overthrow the communist government there on our doorstep ... and a sniper tried to take some of us out, unsuccessfully. I was a PAO onboard a ship in the Persian Gulf during the largest naval battle since World War II, Operation Praying Mantis, in 1988. For four months I was the U.S. spokesperson during the overthrow of a thug ruler in Haiti in 1994. I was the spokesman and public information adviser to the Supreme Allied Commander of Europe for two years, during some challenging times in the mid-90s (Bosnia, Kosovo). I was the PAO for U.S. Special Operations Command from 1997-1999. I was the PAO for the U.S. Army in the Pentagon from 1999-2001, working with national and international media on some of the most visible crises our Nation and our armed forces faced.

Why is this important for you to know? Because I can honestly say that I know how the newspapers of Jefferson's day ... and of today ... work, and I know what drives their editors and reporters to do what they do. Not a whole lot has changed when it comes to the underlying foundational make up of news-covering organizations.

Are some biased? Of course. I wrote a paper in my journalism master's course on bias by the *New York Times* during the Vietnam War. In some ways they *were* biased and in others they were very balanced and totally professional. I've studied closely the workings of the media for decades now and how media, in general, function when it comes to covering our presidents, our political seasons, our political parties, our Congress, etc. Whoever is in the seat in the Oval Office, at any given time, will be scrutinized by most media. Are media, in general, more liberal in their approach to their topics? Possibly, but you could find many scholarly studies that will give you multiple perspectives on that debate.

My view, based on my many years of observing this phenomenon, is that there are enough different types of media in existence today that we can truly get a balanced view of things. To get that balanced view, however, requires intentionally taking the time to survey the multiple media outlets that cover today's world, and then decide for yourself. The bottom line for *most* media (and you can find exceptions to any "rule") is that finding the truth, about any newsworthy activity, drives the media organization owners, which drives media editors, which drives media reporters. I'll qualify this statement somewhat by saying there is an old adage ... *if it bleeds ... it leads ...* In other words, finding the sensational story will get readers to read/view the news organization's story. That is true to an extent, but I can safely say that for most media ... *it's all about finding the truth!*

I spend a good chunk of my days (and I'm now retired, so I can afford more time than most) surveying many different media outlets, trying to find all aspects of any given topic, or issue, or controversy. Then I decide what I am going to believe. Finding the truth is my ultimate goal. It should be the ultimate goal of all of us, before we make judgments about anyone or anything.

Is there a spiritual, faith-based link to any of the words I have written so far? Well, I've spent years studying God's Word and one of the things I've yet to discover—even when Googling about it—is specific guidance on newspapers, reporting, mass media ... or social media, the huge media phenomenon of today. I do believe, however, that Jesus spoke a powerful word in John 8:32: "Then you will know the truth, and the truth will set you free."

Can we apply this wonderful passage to the topic at hand? That's up to you. I can. And this passage also implores me, as a Christ-follower and as a registered Independent in the State of Florida, to spend more time seeking His Truths, than wallowing in the messy politics of the day.

I will seek the truth in all matters of government and politics, as they apply to me, my family, and my life here on earth. I will also endeavor to spend *more quality time* each day in God's Word, seeking His Truths and applying them to my life, than surveying the media each day about the political controversies of the hour.

I found this quote from Billy Graham in the Foreword to a book by the esteemed English journalist, the late Malcom Muggeridge, in his book, ***Christ and the Media***. I'll close with it. I cannot wrap this up any more profoundly than this quote by Dr. Graham. I'd just simply say ... don't get so wrapped up, embroiled in, and worried about how our news media do their important jobs. Instead, step back, take a deep breath ... and listen carefully to multiple views presented by media. Find the truth, as best you perceive it. *Then stay in God's Word. Know and experience His Truth. Let's all apply it to our daily lives.*

Here is the quote from Billy Graham:

> "In a sense the problem of the media is but a symptom of a deeper problem—the problem of the human heart, alienated from God. Only the radical transformation Christ brings will ever be able to solve this fundamental problem. Malcom Muggeridge has seen this clearly, and I am thankful that he reminds us once again of the only hope for the human race—Jesus Christ, our Lord."

Barry Willey, *"Thoughts on the News Media"*

*****

Author's Note: **Barry Willey** and I have been friends for many years, dating back to the early 2000s. His is a remarkable career of presenting truth, dealing with varieties of news media as a spokesperson for the United States Army during some of our nation's past wars and conflicts, including Granada 1983, Haiti 1994. He has been and currently is an investor in lives for the cause of Christ. He was a staff representative at West Point for the Officer's Christian Fellowship from 2005-2009. He and his wife, Barb, and I conducted a cadet training retreat just outside of the United States Military Academy, New York, West Point, and he was instrumental in opening the door for me to consult with the Directorate of Admissions at West Point. We've travelled to Gettysburg, Pennsylvania, and spent quality time at his homes, in Virginia, and just outside of West Point. It was an honor to publish two of Barry's books in 2015: ***Out of the Valley * An Amazing Life Story That Can Help You Make Good Choices and Leave an Eternal Legacy*** and ***Extreme Investing * Changing the World One Believer at a Time***.

Please see this website to view and order these: **www.investingthatmatters.com**. Barry is a role model and an inspiration to me. I respect him highly. He is a brother in Christ.

Chapter 8
Compassion and Common Ground for Those Affected by Crisis

Bud Hendrickson, Industrial Engineering and Maintenance Management
Author *Enjoy Your Journey * Ten Bedrock Truths to Improve Everything About You*

August 8, 2020

I find it amazing how life has unfolded and brought new meaning and truth to my life's journal that I eventually put into book form with the help of Glen Aubrey and Creative Team Publishing. In the chapter Bedrock Truth #10, All Things Work Together for Good to Those Who Love God, I started the chapter with the quote from Benjamin Franklin: "The only absolutes in life are death and taxes." What I was getting at is that trials and difficult times come into everyone's life. The severity, the timing, and the specifics may be different but there are challenges for everyone to face.

That was so true in 2020! COVID-19 had an impact on probably all 7 billion people on the planet.

I find it amazing that a virus could start in one part of the world, travel over numerous oceans, across very large land masses, and affect the rich, the poor, male, female, all races, urban, rural, and the list could go on. But not all had been affected in the same way, and with this variance many very strong positions emerged. Among them:

1. Close down the economy and shelter in place to save lives.
2. Only essential businesses were allowed to continue operations.

That begs the question: What is essential? And the answer varies according to each person's definition. There was a need to open up the economy as millions in just the United States alone became unemployed, not to mention the unknown number of small businesses that were shut down. Many of these businesses may never reopen due to financial ruin caused by the closure and future uncertainty of the COVID-19 pandemic.

There still exist many unknowns about how the virus will affect the health of many in the future. There was a race to find treatments and a vaccine while the virus seemed to continue to mutate. With all the challenges the virus brought, how to open and manage the economy continued to be hotly debated.

These questions persisted:

1. Do we open schools and have sporting events in the fall of 2020?
2. Is it becoming safer to travel and fly to destinations for pleasure and business?
3. Is it becoming safe to worship, get married, or mourn the death of a loved one in a group setting?

How may our "normal" life be forever changed by the pandemic events we confronted?

Having been a football linebacker and acquiring the skills to take in information quickly and make rapid decisions, I have to say that these pandemic-related events had left me wondering what the *truth* is, what *decisions* need to be made, and most importantly, how I should *respond* to other people in the actions I take.

I admired the commitment and dedication of our President and his task forces since the decisions dealing with COVID-19 were major; and there had been little data or history upon which to base them. Anyone who has had to make tough decisions may not agree with all the decisions that are rendered but I have to admire the courage it takes to make them.

There have been many successes to celebrate and honor, like the rapid choice to limit travel, ramp up production of personal protective equipment (PPE) and ventilators, quick development of hospital beds early on, not knowing if the medical resources would be overrun with infected people. Sharing information, tapping into talents and resources to quickly have treatment available, and best practices to minimize loss of life were just a few of the successes.

I would also say we have had many examples from which to learn. For example:

1. How to protect the most vulnerable
2. How to keep people safe who are doing essential jobs or need to work
3. The importance of every citizen being diligent of their own safety with the virus as long as it lingers
4. It is not only our own health that can be affected by our choices, but the health of others we come in contact with and, by extension, those who they come in contact with and who they come in contact with!

In 2013 my first wife of 26 years was diagnosed with Stage 4 colon cancer. One thing I learned early on is that sometimes the treatment can be as bad, or worse, than the disease you are fighting. I got the same feeling when I looked at some of the proposed actions to address the pandemic.

I have compassion as there were many that were very vulnerable to the disease, and we've known it can be deadly. I also realized that shutting down the economy and sheltering in place had as big or bigger impacts on lives. The economic earthquakes have hit many people. Earthquakes come quickly and usually without warning, and there is no totally effective preventative preparation for an earthquake. Is that not what happened with the COVID-19 pandemic? There was little to no warning and few preparations could be made once we became aware. Many people were affected severely without any bad decisions on their parts.

My go-to Bible verse became the foundation I used to cope with my wife's terminal illness starting in 2013, and a major injury I sustained in 2016 where I fell ten feet and broke seven ribs and my collar bone. That go-to verse is this: "And we all know that all things work together for good to them that love God, to them who are the called according to his purpose." Romans 8:28 (KJV)
King James Version of the Holy Bible, Public Domain

I purposefully use my free will to pray to God about what can I learn going through the challenges and difficult times I face. I focus on how I can become more Christlike; enduring the challenges I confront.

I have become much more compassionate, understanding, and respectful of the difficulties chronically ill patients deal with. I gained utmost respect for people, like my wife, who stared death in the face with peace, and showed appreciation for the medical professionals who served her until death. I admire more the people who have chronic pain most of their lives and smiles on their faces. I have gained an understanding of what it feels like to be isolated from others as I did not work and could not drive for about three months after my injury. I had an end in sight for my pain and discomfort, but many do not.

As I look at the crazy and challenging times we have gone through and will continue to go through for who knows how long, I am again praying to God: *"How do I become more Christlike and be a good representative of God and his love?"* What God has put on my heart is that there were valid needs and issues of people in the various issues surrounding the pandemic and other crises we are all dealing with.

In my book, ***Enjoy Your Journey * Ten Bedrock Truths to Improve Everything About You,*** I wrote about the **power of diversity** in managing complex/or important situations: "Plan wisely before moving forward."

The best plan often requires acquiring and evaluating the opinion, action, and competence of more than one qualified individual. The power that allows more effective decision making comes from the Common Ground or Mutual understanding as shown in the figure on the next page.

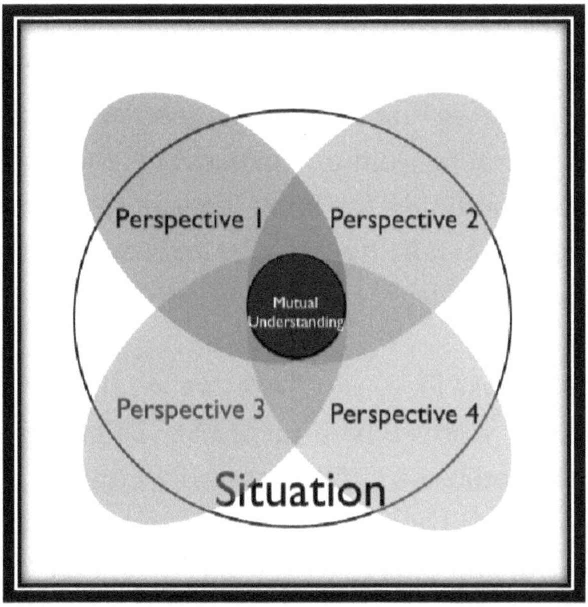

© 2016 Bud Hendrickson in ***Enjoy Your Journey* * *Ten Bedrock Truths to Improve Everything About You***

The next question is this: "How do we find Common Ground and Mutual Understanding in divisive times?" Name-calling and looking through the rearview mirror to find fault are not the answers, yet we see wrong answers play out every day on multiple media channels and possibly in our real lives, too, no matter the crisis. We need to look through the rearview mirror to celebrate accomplishments or learn from past actions/results that will allow us to look through the windshield to better navigate through these challenging issues moving forward.

Finding common ground requires us to reach out to people with other perspectives and expertise, to find out the real issues they are confronting and what their ideas are for dealing with the challenges. Then, coming from their perspectives, can we find areas of common needs and benefits where we can share from our experience and expertise the actions and solutions we may consider? *With identified common ground hopefully there is trust and respect that will allow conversation to continue.*

As Christians, let's ask: "Are we willing to look into someone else's world where there may be effective actions different from our own?" "Will we be willing to be open to conversations that could form the catalyst that allows even more powerful and effective solutions to emerge?" If we can consider these options, imagine the trust and strength of relationships that could be built providing foundations upon which to build even more successes in dealing with the issues that lie ahead for all of us!

But how do we develop the mindset to be the constructive and supportive person to allow common ground to develop? Again, I go to the Bible. The passage is known as the two greatest commandants when Jesus said in Mathew 22:37-40 (KJV): 37 Jesus said unto him, "Thou shalt love the Lord thy God with all thy heart, and with all thy soul, and with all thy mind. 38 This is the first and great commandment. 39 And the second is like unto it, thou shalt love thy neighbor as thyself. 40 On these two commandments hang all the law and the prophets."

Who is "thy neighbor?" All people we come in contact with!! Could you imagine a world if all lived by these commandments and obeyed them? *The love of God gives us the motivation and power to change how we act and behave based on God's truth. By loving our neighbor, we are motivated to make decisions in the best interest not only for ourselves but also consider the needs of others.*

If we choose to take the first step in considering the needs of all, hopefully that choice will be a catalyst for actions and solutions for others with whom we are dealing. My prayer for our country and world is that we *don't* go back to the old normal. I pray that we reprioritize our lives and commit more strongly to our relationship with God, self, family, friends, and co-workers. I pray that people will look beyond themselves for common ground and mutual understanding, so that improved, more effective solutions can be found for the greatest benefit of all, no matter what crises we may face.

Does that mean there will be no future deaths from the presence of COVID-19? Will there be no future jobs lost as a result of COVID-19? No. But what I do believe is that *we continue to protect the most vulnerable, get people back to work using best practices of masks, distancing, hand washing, sanitizing high touch areas, and temperature readings that have allowed many businesses that were deemed essential to remain open and keep their employees safe during the pandemic.*

Bud Hendrickson, "Compassion and Common Ground for Those Affected by Crisis"

Could schools open up in the fall of 2020 and beyond? I think if you look at what essential businesses and healthcare professionals have done there may be solutions to allow these openings to happen, while keeping teachers and students safe.

We need to be open and use the power of common ground and the love of God to get there.

To a stronger future for all! Who knows what that will look like? *But with God, most of the time, the possibilities are beyond our comprehension.*

To a stronger future for all!
Who knows what that will look like?
But with God, most of the time, the possibilities are beyond our comprehension.

*****

Author's Note: **Bud Hendrickson** and I have engaged in multiple professional and personal associations down through the years, including my professional consulting with two of his employers, building core and leadership teams, and with his church through developing programming arts teams (teams of people who provide music, media, drama, technical services, support services, stage design, and artistic direction for church services and meetings). When I got to know Bud early on, I became fascinated by a one-word expression with which he closed every email he composed, no matter the contents. That word was "Enjoy." This is his philosophy of life and his outlook, regardless of circumstances. When we worked together on his book, ***Enjoy Your Journey * Ten Bedrock Truths to Improve Everything About You,*** "Enjoy" became a part of the title of the book. To "enjoy" is the choice of a positive attitude, both given and received. His book (hardcover or softcover) contains God-birthed truths you will likely desire to incorporate into your life, and the lives of your family members. His book is a solid resource for you and yours. **Order the book at this website: www.EnjoyandImprove.com**

Chapter 9
Content Whatever the Circumstances

John Emra, CEO, Life Is Full of Choices
Author *Cornerstones and Core Needs of Growing Kids*, *Parenting from the Top of the Mountain*, and *Seven Steps to the Top of the Mountain*

August 10, 2020

"... for I have learned to be content in whatever the circumstances..."
Philippians 4:11b
New American Standard Bible (NASB)

COVID-19 in 2020 changed all of our circumstances. My hope is to help all of us understand what Paul meant when he said, "whatever the circumstances..."

My wife, Sheryl, and I started working in East Los Angeles with gang kids and their families in 1986. We developed an after-school program. We called it, *The Center*. Our focus was to keep kids in school, off the street, and out of the gangs.

We accomplished this purpose by building relationships with the kids and teaching them some very simple principles.

The most important one being: "Life Is Full of Choices."

This sentence developed into the central theme of what became the "Three Cornerstones" that we used to change young lives. Read about the transformation of kids' lives in ***Cornerstones and Core Needs of Growing Kids.*** (Please see: www.LifeIsFullOfChoices.org.)

The First Cornerstone became: *Life is full of choices, and the choices I make today will determine the qualities of my life both now and in the future.*

We did everything we could to imprint this saying on their young lives. We said it hundreds of times a day. We painted that slogan on the wall. When we weren't saying it, we were pointing to the words on the wall.

We believed that if we could convince the children of this truth (that their choices determined their qualities) then we could create an everlasting impact on their lives.

It worked.

When we were teaching Bible Club, one of the tools we used was to take the scripture lesson or story and input the word "choices" or its synonyms wherever it fit.

For example, John 3:16 became: *"For God chose to love the world so much that he chose to give His one and only son, that whoever chooses to believe on Him would not perish, but is choosing to have eternal life."*

We discovered the Bible took on new power for these kids when we presented it in a way they could understand, relate to, and incorporate into their lives.

I believe that is true for you and me as well.

Choices are important. I have to realize what my choices are and how making any one choice will impact my life.

The Second Cornerstone became: *Life is full of choices and the choices I make today can affect the circumstances of my life and other people's lives both now and in the future.*

As we talked to kids about the result of their choices, we differentiated between the qualities and the circumstances that would grow out of their choices. We spent quite a bit of time illustrating the differences between them, and how they related to the choices they were making in life.

We watched two brothers start middle school; one chose to become part of a gang and the other chose to study and distance himself from the gang.

That one choice would determine much of the rest of their lives.

The qualities of my life are what I choose. I control them and the consequences of choosing them are mine to deal with. They cannot be chosen for me and once they are chosen, they cannot be taken from me. I can give them up—but they cannot be taken.

For example, "joy" is a quality. It can be so much a part of me that it permeates my whole life. Everyone I meet can go away talking about how happy, content, and joyful I am. No one can make me sad. I can choose to become sad or sorrowful and give up my badge of joy, but no one has the power over me to make me sad.

Being a thief is also a quality. It is negative, but qualities come as either positive or negative. If I choose to be a thief, no one will trust me. Later in life I can choose to develop the quality of honesty, but replacing one quality with another takes time. For me to develop the new quality takes some time and it takes even more time for other people to see that new quality within me.

A circumstance, however, is given to me or can be taken from me. My choices can affect my circumstance but I have very little control over the circumstance.

Most of our time explaining this to the kids with whom we worked was spent trying to get them to see that a circumstance, while important for life, was not what we wanted to build our lives around.

Also, they needed to realize that qualities and circumstances, while quite similar, were different in that I had control over one and over the other I had no control.

Some of the kids chose to break into *The Center*. They got caught on the premises and then they were going to jail. Their choice to break in resulted in the circumstance of jail time. The quality they would develop from this choice is "outlaw."

Circumstances include my wife, my kids, my church, my job, the money in my bank account, the car I drive; all of these were either given to me or can be taken from me.

If I build my life around one of these, or even a combination of these circumstances, I am setting myself up to be disappointed because someone can take away the central themes of my life.

I was working with a group of teenagers when I said that even my life was a circumstance. One of the teenagers disagreed with me and said; "What if I pulled out a gun and shot you in the head right now? How does that fit with what you are saying?" I said, "That just proves my point. My life would be over. You would have taken it from me. I wouldn't like losing it in that way, but it shows that my life is a circumstance."

I have given you, the readers of this book, all of this about choices as a way of explanation—an introduction if you will, so we can look at COVID-19 and other crises <u>through the lens of choices</u>.

I can choose to become joyful. I can choose to develop an attitude of peacefulness. I can choose to become faithful. I can even choose to develop a loving spirit for those around me.

All of those positive choices would constitute a great legacy to leave behind!

As a Christian, my life is not my own. My life belongs to God; it is for Him to use. We often like to think that we control our own lives, but the reality is when I gave my life to Him, I gave Him control over every choice I make.

For a life dedicated to God and filled with peace, faithfulness, and love, the consequence is heaven.

That is the condition in which Paul found himself when he wrote to the Philippians.

Or consider the story of Stephen in the New Testament. He talks about the choice he made to preach to the masses about Jesus. He could have just walked away, but God gave him a message to preach, and boy, did he preach! The consequence was: they stoned him. He died.

Now my life may be 60, 70, or 80+ years long. Compared to eternity that lifespan is but a grain of sand on the beaches of the world's timeline—but it is the only grain of sand I know, so I want to hold on to it. That is normal; that is human. But, like Steven, we are called to be more than human.

No rational person wants to die. People commit suicide to escape the mess of life, but Steven did not commit suicide. He was following God's plan for his life; he died and went to heaven. We can choose to see death as a negative outcome, but to Steven it was a positive experience.

What a legacy he left behind!

We are called to be God's ambassadors on earth.

And as long as He wants me here, I need to represent Him.

That span of time could be a day, a week, a year, or multiple years!

That is the issue; we simply don't know.

We all would like to be here for a long time. None of us wanted to die from the COVID-19 virus, but what does God want?

I could spend my days experiencing fear and worry about catching it, or I can trust God to protect me from this illness, and if I contract it, to take care of me. *The choice is mine!*

Look at all of life as a composite. Life can include:

1. The financial uncertainty with the stock market and/or our jobs
2. The rioting we see
3. The next elections
4. Racial tensions in the world (remember: my race was given to me at birth so it is a circumstance)
5. What the news media thinks is important and is focusing on
6. Even my desire to see people who are important to me.

Can I trust God for all of these circumstances?

I will be more composed, more focused, better able to deal with life, and more useful to Him as I focus on His priorities for my life.

Remember: these circumstances are not new. The idea of a Christian giving up his or her life for his or her faith is as old as Christianity itself, and we should not look at what we are losing but what we are gaining. God knows all things. Can I trust Him to use the circumstances of my life for His glory? Can I trust Him to use the circumstances of my death for His glory?

> *I will be more composed, more focused,*
> *better able to deal with life, and more useful to Him as I focus on His priorities for my life.*

Here is the part we have all been waiting for—the conclusion.

If we looked at COVID-19 as a horrible event, then we were not seeing it for what it was.

COVID-19 was a circumstance. Its presence gave us the opportunity to be more than conquerors! *We can be conquerors instead of victims in any crisis.*

> *We can be conquerors instead of victims.*

The reason I wrote this was to illustrate this truth: we have a choice.

We can choose to dwell in dark and depressing aspects of death or the potential of death, or we can choose to see death as a graduation of sorts. We can see any current circumstance as a signpost to point us to God.

John Emra, "Content Whatever the Circumstances"

Remember what Paul wrote to the Thessalonians:

Now may the Lord of peace Himself continually grant you peace in every circumstance. The Lord be with you all.
2 Thessalonians 3:16 (NASB)

We do not choose our circumstances – we can only choose how we respond to them.

The choice is yours. Choose wisely.

*****

Author's Note: **John and Sheryl Emra** and I became acquainted in 2008 when both of them were part of a ministry organization in Los Angeles, where I consulted with them as they served the people of the Inner City. John asked me about publishing. Once I learned about their work with inner city kids at *The Center,* my earnest desire became to publish his story. His concepts of "life is full of choices" really took shape at *The Center*, and literally have impacted thousands of lives across the country. I have experienced John's passion and presentation as a missionary to those he is called to reach, in several different venues including churches, training seminars, and a Rotary service club audience. His books are profound and entertaining, as well as packed with great advice and instructions one can put to practical use in any circumstance. I recommend these books to all parents and guardians who want to parent better and "do it right." You will find his books to be informative, effective, and intriguing. They "hit the mark" of what effective parenting needs to be and what kids are all about. Make good choices; observe and participate in the welcome results. Purchase his three books here: **www.LifeIsFullOfChoices.org.** This purchase is a worthwhile investment for you and your entire family.

Chapter 10
Who Is My Neighbor?

James Patton, Former V.P. Operations, Absolute Security

August 31, 2020

"Who is my neighbor?" Jesus gave a very simple two-part answer to *all* the real root problems that plague us. Let's address just one aspect as an example of an urgent symptom of the underlying cancer of self-centeredness and fear of scarcity, the seriousness of a single cell or a small gang of cells that will grow if unchecked, and that is the real situation that sickens and is killing us.

Just like we do with our individual human bodies we must do as a body of human beings. While we must rapidly realize, respond, and remedy general symptoms such as racism and the resulting specific outgrowth symptoms such as injustice, to really heal and be in great health we go to the cancer source. The word of God provides the simple prescription for the solution to a multitude of manifestations.

Remember and reflect Almighty God's love to us and through us. His words are commands that we each must easily implement immediately.

God's two key commands are recorded in Matthew 22:37-40:

> 37 Jesus replied, "'Love the Lord your God with all your heart, soul, and mind.' 38-39 This is the first and greatest commandment. The second most important is similar: 'Love your neighbor as much as you love yourself.' 40 All the other commandments and all the demands of the prophets stem from these two laws and are fulfilled if you obey them. Keep only these and you will find that you are obeying all the others." (TLB)
>
>

The first part of the Great Commandment is to love God. God (the Almighty Creator of the universe who showed His love for us by sacrificing His Son to save us) is our compass. If you left San Diego to visit a friend in New York City and you were only one degree off when you departed, you would not only miss reaching your friend in New York City by 40 miles; you would be so far off that you could not even see New York City, which is one of the largest cities in the world. That's needlessly "a little lost," don't you think? A compass can't be ignored for true undistracted direction to reach our desired destiny. Loss: from The White House to The Jail House and through Our House.

When we obey the first Great Commandment, to love God, our obedience sets our course correctly. In the example of missing New York City by 40 miles, we see a graphic illustration of what is known as the "1 in 60 rule." In air navigation, the "1 in 60 rule" states that "if a pilot has traveled sixty miles off course, that error in the track of one mile equates to approximately a one degree error in heading, and proportionately more for larger errors." (*Wikipedia Encyclopedia* *) If you look at any audit of wrongdoing, or crime, there is almost always a pattern of being "off," usually seen going way back. It typically started with a slight and unchecked deviance and grew the farther it was allowed to go, until predictable disaster occurred. When evil is excused then evil is escalated.

> Ecclesiastes 8:11:
> 11 When the sentence for a crime is not quickly carried out, people's hearts are filled with schemes to do wrong.

The second part of the Great Commandment is like the first. Jesus commanded us to love our neighbors as ourselves. Ask yourselves regarding any wrongful action or condition:

1. "Would you want it done to you?"
2. "How long would you be willing to be oppressed?"
3. What if "Justice for all" meant for all but you, and anyone like you? By virtually every meaningful

measure, the System is sick: No Justice: No Peace. Know Justice: Know Peace.

4. Justice can't mean "just us." What is vitally required is urgent equity in every underlying area.

What if you painfully and vividly knew that the Declaration of Independence is often implemented like this: "We hold these truths to be self-evident, that all (*except you*) are created equal, that they are endowed by our Creator with certain unalienable (undeniable/undisputed) Rights that among these are Life, Liberty and the Pursuit of Happiness (*except for you*)?" A challenge is to accept this fact: huge race disparity consequences and deaths still remain; yes, it's really that bad. In truth: "Group holding gun has a different view from person facing the gun. Especially if they or their loved ones have been hunted and hung before."

This is not an incident; it is an indication. We may tape over the "fuel empty" light but the tank still runs out of gas. Why not enforce verified total accountability and equity? To impose or allow: "Trust us not to stack the deck any worse…" or "let's leave it rigged" inflames injury even more.

The Bob Dylan song, "The Times They Are A Changing" summarizes the following fact: in 1960 the U.S. Non-Hispanic White population was 89%; in 2016 it was 61%, and by 2060 it will be 40%.

(U.S. Census Bureau Population by Race at census.gov)

The "who is my neighbor?" part is easy because it refers to everybody *except* us. Jesus offered an example (recorded in Luke 10:25-37) of a person who was attacked, beaten, and robbed. People walked by and everyone had an excuse as to why they couldn't help. Finally, a stranger (ironically from a people group, a culture/race their people despised) stopped and took care of everything that might be required to aid the injured person. Jesus asked his listener, "Who was a neighbor to the person who fell into the hands of robbers?" This listener had now learned the key life lesson and rightly replied: "The person who showed mercy." Jesus commanded: "Go and do likewise."

Here is an agricultural question with a life application answer: What is the best way to tell if a tree is a peach tree? You are right! Judge it by its fruit. Peach roots grow peach trees, which bear peach fruit, which have peach seeds, to repeat the process. Even if the tree has a big new sign that shouts, "I am an Orange tree," it's still a peach tree. It's the same with people.

Glen Aubrey is my very dear brother whom I first met about 33 years ago in a youth ministry. Outwardly we are very different: he is White and I am Black. In 2011 he won an Emmy ® Award for music, and I still can't carry a tune even with an 18-wheel truck and a bunch of Teamsters.

Glen is very polished and I am more pointed. We have many differences from each other. Yet what brings us close is what we have in common: it is a love of God, and loving and caring about others as we love and care for ourselves. Glen taught me that "People are more important than programs or projects." That's true when we put others first before ourselves. That's when we value their viewpoint as *the* reality. Instead of saying: "I'm sorry if you were offended," instantly and intentionally we say instead: "What I said and/or did was offensive. I am ashamed and sorry that I hurt you. How can I make it right?" Then we must *do*: not just *say* what is required.

Twenty-one police officers (mostly LAPD) participated (four were active and seventeen as accomplices stood watch and were equally liable) in brutalizing Rodney King. A Taser was used on him *twice*, his skull was fractured, his jaw broken, his liver busted, eleven bones were broken, and he suffered brain damage and more, yet all those officers felt comfortable committing this brutalization, knowing that there would be no consequences. Even though they *knew* they were being recorded on their own dash cameras plus their own body cameras and by passersby; yet both cops and community knew that nothing would be done about it because it was so common to their culture. It was not until an uprising that anything was done. Even then the officers were not punished for Assault with a Deadly Weapon or even misconduct for abusing their authority. Only two were sentenced to a mere 30 months in jail for violating King's civil rights.
(See Rodney King, Wikipedia.com*)

The racist message was not misunderstood. Everyone knew, said, and did exactly what they meant. That message was received and that message must be repulsed.

Two weeks after the Rodney King incident (and only a week before the verdict), a Korean-American shopkeeper, Soon Ja Du, assaulted and then murdered a fifteen-year old African-American girl. The child customer was shot in the back of the head because the shopkeeper claimed she thought the child, Latasha Harlins, was stealing a bottle of orange juice. The racially motivated merchant was holding the juice behind the counter and the child was three feet away and leaving the store with money in hand which she had brought to buy the juice. Video tape recorded all and there were two eyewitnesses. The child was dead. What was the shopkeeper's penalty after conviction? Instead of adhering to the Jury, Probation Officer, and California Penal Codes which recommended sixteen years in prison for voluntary manslaughter with the use of a gun enhancement, Soon Ja Du was fined only $500. (See Killing of Latasha Harlins, Wikipedia.com*)

A week later the same Judge sentenced someone to thirty days in jail for just kicking a dog. Too often we observe graphic illustrations of the disparity of the value of life of black people.
(See Joyce Karlin, Wikipedia.com*).

These are just some classic, well-known documented examples of the still ongoing blatant lack of justice in the justice system and other areas cancer-infected and corrupted both individually and institutionally.

These representative examples are not just about civil rights (based on society's desires): it is about *all of our* human rights (nobody has a right to deny it). The lead police detective (Mark Fuhrman) in the O.J. Simpson first degree murder trial was convicted *of felony perjury in a death penalty case per California law*. He was fined only $200 and got to retire with full pension payments and honors. As a result of Fuhrman's symbolic actions, his paid net worth is $4,000,000. (WealtyPersons.com)

Darkness can't exist if we keep enough light on everywhere. Tragically, "I can't breathe…" (George Floyd's gasping and dying words) is still happening.

Darkness can't exist if we keep enough light on everywhere.

All of us are in this together.
Racism is a crisis, but we know what to do to cure it.
Love God, and love our neighbors as ourselves.

Humans have a heritage of being able to make a choice and a change. Nine years ago, I was run over by a truck while working as a Security Guard. I went from being a recent Police Academy Graduate plus a uniformed San Diego Police volunteer with a great future, to being crippled and in a wheelchair. I quickly discovered there was no insurance.

Government agencies exist that are mandated and funded to help in circumstances like this; yet in this case each agency claimed they were the "payer of last resort." This meant that no real resources were given to me: I was mainly "referred" (told "go-away") to see somebody else: a loop of recurring inaction.

In spite of all this, some people chose to decide that there was something that *they* would do and they made the difference (although I can't go into the details right now: thank you!)

Just as we are grateful our one human body has synergy from diverse parts (... we can't walk on our eyeballs), so, too, we all are a part of our one human race body. With your help this truth becomes clear: when we make it through the testing, we will have a great testimony *together.*

When we make it through the testing, we will have a great testimony *together.*

A great thing about the Bible is that God wrote down reminders to help us remember some All-Stars at their finish, and we also see how God worked through situations to shape them (and us) for bigger successes, setting a precedent. For example: David faced Goliath, Moses had to confront the Red Sea, Mary experienced Immaculate Conception, Queen Esther was first kidnapped, Peter had to get out of the boat in a storm to walk on water when Jesus called to him.

Afford to love: we are agents of The Almighty! God said, "Let there be light…" (Genesis 1:3) and He created all the stars (Genesis 1:16). "Kornreich used a very rough estimate-of 10 trillion galaxies in the universe. Multiplying that by the Milky Way's estimated 100 billion stars (in just our one galaxy) results in a very large number indeed: 1,000,000,000,000,000,000,000,000 stars, or a '1' with 24 zeros after it. Kornreich emphasized that number is likely a gross underestimation, as more detailed looks at the universe will show even more galaxies."
(Dr. David Kornreich, Founder of the "Ask an Astronomer" service at Cornell University * per Space.com)

No room (scarcity)? It's a fact: 63% of us live on 4% of U.S land.
(Census.gov)

God plans opportunity and obligation to move us upward from F.E.A.R (False Evidence Appearing Real), by F.A.I.T.H. (Full Assurance In The Holy Spirit), to work as a T.E.A.M. (Together Everyone Achieves More).
(Original sources of these acronyms are unknown.)

Be encouraged and become empowered: read Hebrews, Chapter 11 aloud.

The two-part command again is this: Jesus replied: "'Love the Lord your God with all your heart, soul, and mind.' This is the first and greatest commandment. The second most important is similar: 'Love your neighbor as much as you love yourself.'" Legal Maxim: "Those who bear the benefit must bear the burden."

The problems and prescription are not new or unique to the United States today; they are urgent for everyone and have been for a long time.

Thanks for your time, attention, and renewed action in obedience to God or at least The Golden Rule: "Do to others as you would have them do to you." (Luke 6:31)

~James Patton, Your Brother

*Details on many of the people and examples cited can be found by Googling and then looking at the Wikipedia.com reference. An advantage you get from Wikipedia Encyclopedia is that it contains context, underlying citations to the original information sources, and links to documentation to independently verify / fact check, to know the truth. It is a good start.

*****

Author's Note: **James Patton** and I have been close friends for over 30 years, as he mentioned. He is a man with big dreams, an unshakeable optimistic attitude, firm resilience and determination, and even more importantly, a deep love for God. We are not of the same race, but we are one in the family of God. He literally is one of my "brothers." He makes me smile. His humor is contagious. James credits me for teaching him many years ago (Thank you, James) but I would like to credit *him* with instructing me about viewpoints and truths inherent in a culture into which I was not born. These characteristics have marked our friendship: we *listen* to each other. We *respect* each other. We *support* each other, and always have done so. I asked James to be a Contributor to this book because of the virtually unmeasurable influence, example, and impact his life has had upon mine. We have shared a lot of time together, and as I think back on it, those memories are indeed precious to me. James, be encouraged, my friend, as you encourage and help others to understand.

Chapter 11
Navigating Uncharted Waters

Sarah S. Falcone, BSN, RN;
Christian Yoga Teacher CYT-200;
Home Healthcare Nurse, Fort Worth, Texas;
Medical Reserve Corps of Tarrant County, Texas

August 12, 2020

During 2020 we were navigating uncharted waters. Well, maybe that's an understatement. For many people that you and I know, the year of 2020 was tragic, painful, or disruptive to say the least. The global pandemic of COVID-19 changed life as we knew it, and I don't think we will truly know to what extent for years to come. Social, economic, and political implications are still yet to be fully realized. For this reason, it can be hard to look ahead to the future.

I certainly had not seen it coming. A slightly older, but much wiser colleague warned me back in February, 2020. We will call her Macy. Macy and I work together as registered nurses providing in-home services to elderly homebound patients. She said something like, "I've got to tell you, I'm really worried about this thing."

And I remember confidently responding, "Oh, I'm not. I heard a podcast saying something about the Influenza pandemic of 1918 wave, and this will probably all die down, too, since summer is coming." Ha! Boy, did I miscalculate that one.

On February 27, 2020, I received an email update from my boss about fourteen confirmed cases of coronavirus in the United States. It outlined the Centers for Disease Control and Prevention (CDC) signs and symptoms to be aware of, requested I check the office stock on N-95 masks, and closed with a statement, "… this is just education … *I am sure it will go by the way* as [Ebola] has. However, it is always our goal to be prepared." Well, at least I wasn't the only one miscalculating. We should have all listened to Macy!

The next day, another email: "… our main supplier is out of masks … we are looking for other suppliers." Okay, so a lot of people were preparing for the worst, I guess. Then just two weeks later another email: "… there have been 423 confirmed cases and 19 deaths, a confirmed case in Frisco, Texas …" It was about this time we heard that kids would not be returning to school from Spring Break. And then came the global toilet paper crisis of 2020. It was about that time that I knew things were getting serious. Just days later I was standing in a Walmart aisle amidst empty shelves, sending group texts to other moms trying to find out where to buy meat and dairy.

This is not a coronavirus 2020 recap or timeline. I just want to make it clear that I certainly didn't see it coming. Like everyone I knew, I had plans for my life: plans for summer trips, birthday parties, a hair appointment.

> "For I know the plans I have for you," declares the LORD, "plans to prosper you and not to harm you, plans to give you hope and a future." Jeremiah 29:11

> "My plans aren't your plans, nor are your ways my ways, says the LORD. Just as the heavens are higher than the earth, so are my ways higher than your ways, and my plans than your plans." Isaiah 58:8, 9 (CEB)
> Common English Bible (CEB), Copyright © 2011 by Common English Bible

I have been a follower of Christ since I was a little girl and I have come to know this to be true: He has plans for me and they are to prosper me, never to harm me, and to give me a hope and a future. Just as the heavens are higher than the earth, so are his plans higher than my plans. He proves it over and over. It's a simple concept.

That doesn't mean it's easy to live by. Simple doesn't mean easy, right? Things can be simple, yet very hard. Like losing weight or saving money, they're simple enough. Take in fewer calories than you burn. Spend less money than you make. But no, it's not easy to commit to, to live by, and to accomplish. It is easy to say you trust God and His lofty plans, but it is sometimes tough to walk in that faith.

It can be hard to trust in a hope and a future when times get tough. The pandemic had magnified heartbreaks like job losses, illness and death, anxiety, and fear. It had also caused a lot of loneliness, isolation, and depression in the name of "social distancing." But even before the pandemic disaster, it wouldn't have taken you long to find tragedy and crises all around: poverty, hunger, natural disasters, and conflict. We live in a fallen world. It has been broken since the Garden of Eden. But those of us who are believers know that Jesus came to redeem us and this world, and in Him we can find hope to sustain us through our journey, until that day when His plan is fulfilled.

> We have this hope as an anchor for the soul,
> firm and secure. Hebrews 6:19a

The Scripture talks about hope as an anchor. After Jesus' death, the early Christians were persecuted by the Jews and the Romans. During the first century a common symbol for Christianity was not a cross; rather, it was an anchor. Believers used the symbol to communicate their faith to other Christians in the form of jewelry, tattoos, even tombstones. It was a sign of strength and a symbol of security, stability, and being grounded. A boat's anchor will hold it down through the stormiest of weather, no matter how severe the storm gets.

On this rough passage through life, when sorrows like sea billows roll, my soul needs an anchor firm and secure. *Thank God we have this hope as an anchor for the soul.*

As I write this, we are somewhere between summer and fall. We've started getting our "sea legs." We are adapting, learning to keep our balance, and finding ways to not feel so seasick onboard the still moving ship. We have found ways to return to routines that we had before with some minor adjustments. Some of the fear and panic has subsided. There are late summer trips being taken, birthday parties with face masks, and hair appointments once again.

All of us "accidental teachers," i.e. parents, prepared for a new school year in the era of coronavirus, amidst arguments about remote learning vs. in-person instruction on the school campuses. I have a daughter in college, one in the class of 2021, and an elementary schooler all affected by uncertain times. Their young lives are unfolding very differently than I would have planned for them. Fear of the unknown multiplied by social media can wreak havoc on the mental health and wellbeing of the next generation. It is a challenge to parent in these times, but even more challenging, I believe, to be growing up in these times.

Please consider this verse of Scripture:

> You planned how many days I would live. You wrote down the number of them in your book before I had lived through even one of them. Psalm 139:16b (NIRV)
>
>

This well-loved psalm reminds me that we were known before we were born. We were each brought into this world at the appointed time, and our heavenly Father already knew what each of our days would look like. Take solace in this thought: before we even lived yesterday and live today, God knew how it would go. And so before we even think about tomorrow, God already knows how it will go.

One theme that came up over and over for me is from the book of Esther. Esther is one of only two books in the Bible without mention of the name of God, yet every event seems to be divinely orchestrated. I enjoy this book: it's an easy read full of drama and plot twists. It's a Biblical soap opera if you will, telling the story of Purim and how the Jews were saved.

Esther is an orphaned Jewish girl raised by her uncle whose beauty finds favor with the king, and then she becomes his queen. She keeps her background secret though, concealing her race from everyone … until! An evil plot to kill all of her people is exposed! Like I said, it's a real page turner.

In one of my favorite scenes Esther's uncle tells her the latest news and the order against the Jews, and urges her to use her royal position to do something about it.

As recorded in the Bible:

> For if you remain silent at this time, relief and deliverance for the Jews will arise from another place, but you and your father's family will perish. And who knows but that you have come to your royal position for such a time as this? Esther 4:14

What a profound thought! And who knows but that *you* have come to *your* royal position for such a time as this? What if you were placed in this specific moment in history, in your city, in your community, in your company, in your school, in your family, in *your home,* for such a time as this? I believe you were.

Isaiah 61 speaks of being called to rebuild, restore, and renew. We are called to proclaim good news, to bind up the broken hearted, and to proclaim freedom for the captives, to release the prisoners, and proclaim the year of the Lord's favor. You are called to comfort those who are mourning, providing for those who are grieving, and to bestow beauty for ashes and garments of praise instead of despair.

You were planted right where you are for this season and you can thrive, instead of just survive. The scripture goes on to say: "They will be called oaks of righteousness, a planting of the LORD for the display of his splendor." Isaiah 61:3b

Oak trees are beautiful and strong trees that can withstand incredibly strong storms, even hurricanes or tornadoes. They have long branches and deep roots.

As any tumultuous time feels like it is trying to toss you about, or like it's throwing your loved ones to and fro, remember that *you were planted in this time with purpose*. Your days have already been written by one who is madly in love with you. Remember your anchor. Those who trust in God's plan are safe and secure. You will not be harmed. Even though we don't know what is next we can look to the future confidently.

> You are called to comfort those who are mourning, provide for those who are grieving, and to bestow beauty for ashes and garments of praise instead of despair. You were planted right where you are for this season and you can thrive, instead of just survive.

*****

Author's Note: **Sarah Falcone** and I became acquainted in February of 2020. We happily attend the same church in North Fort Worth, Texas. In a word, she is giver of hope and truth. She possesses unshakeable confidence in God's provision. When we met, she was serving me graciously, and I was deeply moved. I invited her then to write a book for Creative Team Publishing to produce, because as you can already tell, she communicates in a style that is gentle yet firm, caring yet impeccably honest, and Biblically accurate. She admonishes all to trust God and obey the calling He has placed on their hearts. For her book, I encouraged her to include Biblical faith and modern medicine. She is an RN, a healthcare professional. She cares deeply for those who benefit from her expertise. What an honor to receive and include her writing here for ***God's Plan Unfolding * Strength and Renewal in Times of Crisis***. Thank you, Sarah!

Chapter 12
A Spoonful of Cookie Dough

Will Hathaway
Police Officer, Patrol Officer,
SWAT (Special Weapons and Tactics) Negotiator,
School Resource Officer, Trainer, Part Time Pastor
Author *What If God Is Like This?*
The Human Side of Christ * Meet the Guy Behind the God,
and *Naked*

August 21, 2020

When it comes to death, we live in a rather sanitized society. People die and we are able to quickly surround the scene, keep others away, then whisk the body off to a mortuary where it is cleaned up, and placed in a casket and then put on display for family and loved ones with a peaceful and tranquil expression, tenderly ushering our dear ones off to the other side.

It's strange really. For as uncomfortable as we are with death, we don't seem to have much of a problem with killing. After all, it dominates our news, entertainment, and video games. And rather innocently at times! For many years one of the most popular genera of novel has been the "murder mystery." But death itself?

Real death, personal death—my eventual death? Those seem to be topics we address with much less enthusiasm. While the concept of death doesn't seem all that intimidating, the reality of it is a completely different story.

Societies throughout history have contrived many different ways of dealing with death, one of the oldest being the advent of religion. At the heart of just about every religion on earth is the topic of death. A friend of mine once posed a question that has haunted me ever since when he asked me, "Do you think religion would even exist if it weren't for death?" I had never thought to view religion (of any kind) from this perspective, but the more I thought about it the more convinced I've become that the great appeal of religion for many of us, is it allows us a place to deposit our fears of death: exchanging those fears for the comforting promise of a utopian life ever after, free of pain and discomfort.

One of the drawbacks I fear is sometimes they can get us so focused on the next life, that we forget to fully embrace the life in which we currently occupy. It was Jesus Himself who pointed out in the famed Lord's Prayer, that our desire should be, "Thy kingdom come," and that "Thy will be done on earth as it is in Heaven." Interesting concepts as the focus of the energies seem not to be achieving entrance into heaven after we die, but to strive to bring it here before we die. Does this, perhaps, play into part of our disconnect with the idea of death? Death in and of itself seems painful enough with its no exceptions policy of eventually claiming us all, ending relationships, and separating loved ones, but perhaps, do we actually increase that pain and trauma with our apathetic interest in addressing the possibility and reality of death in a more constructive way?

As a first responder, almost half my life now has been dedicated to being one of those "sanitizers." I am part of the group that helps deal with the messy realities of death, so as to shield the rest of society from its burden. It's impossible to do such a job without having to at least come to terms with your own mortality and come to the realization as to the fragility of life.

Every day I would leave for work and in the back of my mind was an ever-present awareness that this could be my final day on the job, and the planet. It was this gentle awareness that caused me to take an extra moment every day to appreciate that hug and kiss to the family a little more. It also caused me to never leave without making sure that little exchange was taking place.

Looking back, I can say there were two major factors that played into my ability not to allow this daily ritual to fade away. The first was the obvious realization that I had a dangerous job and bad things can occur. But the other was the regular interactions with death as a result of the work. Car accidents, drownings, medical issues, homicides, tragedies of various kinds were always there to consistently remind me that life is something that is fragile for all of us, not just those of us with dangerous jobs. The vast majority of deaths I've encountered involved regular people simply living their lives when something unexpected and terrible occurred, ending that life.

It didn't take long before I began to notice the idea of a "dangerous job" was a little bit of an illusion, in that the death scenes I was often responding to involved people with non-dangerous jobs doing non-dangerous things. In the end, it turned out to be a blessing for me as I was forced to examine the reality of death in a much deeper and more personal way than I may have had I chosen another career path.

A second appreciation that has emerged from this line of thinking as I've aged has been the appreciation of how temporary everything in life is. While life and death are obviously the dominate philosophical elements here, one of the related realizations is that life is broken down into subcategories, experiences that we have daily opportunities to embrace, but often allow to pass by unnoticed. During the course of a life, friends come and go, neighbors move, favorite restaurants close, kids grow up, new cars eventually break down, and our bodies once capable of certain physical feats eventually weaken to the point that even the basic function of walking becomes difficult.

I sometimes wonder: "Is it the lack of appreciation of the brevity of life's moments that increases our struggles to accept the conclusion of those moments when they come?" When we mourn the loss of either certain stages of life, or on the extreme level, the losses of people in our lives, is part of that pain the realization we didn't take full advantage of the time we *did* have? Is part of our struggle with missing people and experiences when they are gone is that we actually first missed them before they were gone? Never fully taking the time to capture the moment and extract the fullness of the experience at hand, our minds wandering elsewhere instead?

When we mourn the loss of either certain stages of life, or on the extreme level, the losses of people in our lives, is part of that pain the realization we didn't take full advantage of the time we *did* have?

I caught myself doing this even as I was writing this chapter. I could hear my kids laughing downstairs as they had decided to make cookies and start a movie. For a moment I was distracted by their laughter as I tried to focus on my writing, only to suddenly realize I was right in the middle of an opportunity to enjoy exactly what I'm currently writing about. My kids will not always be home to laugh and make cookies, and I was taking that for granted. Someday it will be silent downstairs as the laughter and cookies will be their childhood memories of long ago. Thankfully I realized this and set the keyboard aside to go down and enjoy the time with them as well as to steal some fresh cookie dough which was delicious.

It saddens me how often I still miss these moments, especially with so many ancient voices crying out through the ages reminding us to capture them. Those who have lived before us discovered all too quickly how easily this experience called life can slip through our fingers. They have etched their warnings over and over on stones and parchments urging us to heed their words, live now, capture the moment, savor the experience, be it joyful or sorrowful, pleasant or foul, beautiful or ugly. All experiences are needed for one to encounter life to the full.

If anything, the reality of death can hold one of two different positions in our lives. It can be a looming, dark, future dread. Or, it can be a constant reminder to savor the right now. As much as we tend to take life for granted, perhaps it's a good thing we don't live forever lest we would never get around to actually savoring anything, and that would be even more tragic than death.

*****

Author's Note: **Will Hathaway** and I have been friends since I was a worship consultant to Monte Vista Church of the Nazarene in Phoenix, Arizona. The year was 1997. Since 2001, Will has worked as a full-time Police Officer and Part-Time Pastor. His roles have included Patrol Officer, SWAT (Special Weapons and Tactics) Negotiator, School Resource Officer, and Trainer for his department. Will's depth of knowledge regarding policing, and his leadership and love for youth in and out of church environments are more than admirable; these traits are indicative of a professional who has a heart for reaching young people for the cause of Christ. Will is also a gifted author of three books which every library should have. His three books, ***What If God Is Like This? The Human Side of Christ * Meet the Guy Behind the God,*** **and *Naked*** can be ordered at **www.will-hathaway.com.**
His writing is superb, and it causes every reader to *think.*

Chapter 13

Restore the American Dream

Larry Wolf
Department Chair of Criminal Justice
University of Antelope Valley, Lancaster, California
Author *A Black and White Decision * Why George Zimmerman Was Found Innocent * Why America Must Honor the Memory of Trayvon Martin*, and *Policing Peace: What America Can Do Now to Avoid Future Tragedies*

August 31, 2020

The optics and reality of George Floyd begging for his life and then being killed was horrific. (May 25, 2020, Minneapolis) The grotesque historic symbolism of a black man pinned to the ground at the neck by a white peace officer's knee started a firestorm of protests not seen since the Rodney King riots and the violent unrest of the 1960s.

The tragedy of his death and the violence and destruction that followed has shaken America to her core.

In light of this disaster we must be willing to ask the tough questions, accept inconvenient truths, and implement difficult solutions.

What can we do to reduce the chances of this type of incident from happening again? How can we end the violence and unrest that threatens our nation? What can we do to restore the hope and promise that is America?

Here are ten actions we can take now to overcome our latest national tragedy and begin to restore the American Dream.

1) Respond to the need first

Black lives matter—period. Anything we do which devalues black lives is wrong. This is what needs to be heard loud and clear when something as horrible as Minneapolis takes place.

The Apostle Paul tells us to "... weep with them who weep." Romans 12:15b (NASB)
New American Standard Bible (NASB) Copyright © 1960, 1962, 1963, 1968, 1971, 1972, 1973, 1975, 1977, 1995 by The Lockman Foundation

Even the tough and adventurous Teddy Roosevelt knew the importance of empathy by virtue of his off quoted statement, "No one cares about how much you know, until they know how much you care."
www.brainyquote.com Theodore Roosevelt Quotes

2) Take the moral high ground—protest peacefully

Dr. Martin Luther King never wavered in his belief that non-violence was the only viable means to achieve his dream. By taking the moral high ground, the difference between right and wrong could not have been clearer and a large majority of Americans embraced his cause.

Hateful, violent tactics disgrace those involved and tend to discredit the legitimacy of any ideology they profess. Often, we are won over more by the actions and morality of people than by their actual message.

"Peacemakers who sow in peace reap the harvest of righteousness." (James 3:18)

3) Have the courage to speak up and tell the truth

Cops not telling the truth or exaggerating wildly, cause a crisis of credibility and are deleterious to the cause of justice. Video-taped incidents have exposed police misconduct and shown some of their stories to be less than truthful. Citizen lies can be at the heart of unjust verdicts in criminal trials.

In the Michael Brown case in Ferguson, Missouri, August 9, 2014, some courageous African American witnesses told the truth even though they had been threatened. They backed up Officer Wilson's account of what had happened. This allowed investigating officials including Attorney

General Eric Holder to conclude that officer Wilson should not be prosecuted.

"Equal justice under the law" promised to our citizens in the 14th Amendment must have truth as its foundation. Without the truth, injustice is sure to follow.

4) Seek the counsel of minority criminal justice professionals

Attorney General Holder found that one of the biggest problems in Ferguson was a significant disparity in the racial makeup of the Ferguson Police Department. There were only two African American peace officers on a force that policed a city that was 67% black. This imbalance was clearly not the recipe for effective community policing.

People of color within the criminal justice system are well positioned to give perspective on racially charged cases. Attorney General Holder, as an African American and a defender of minority rights, came to Ferguson with every intention of prosecuting officer Wilson had there been evidence to support a prosecution.

In the end, more of the evidence provided primarily by African American witnesses, showed that Officer Wilson's actions appeared to be justified under the circumstances.

Often because of all of the circumstances present, many tragic incidents are clearly not criminal. Sometimes justice will come in the civil realm. However inadequate they might seem; monetary judgements often are the best that can be done to help people start their lives over after a tragedy.

Whenever there are injuries or death and questionable police behavior, having minorities involved in the process helps with both the appearance and reality of justice. We must continue to make minority hiring a priority with the goal of having the racial makeup of a police force mirror the community they serve.

"Acquire wisdom! Acquire understanding! Do not forget nor turn away from the words of my mouth. Do not forsake her, and she will guard you, love her, and she will watch over you." Proverbs 4:5-6 (NASB)

5) Provide hope amidst the hopelessness

A distinguished friend of mine once spoke at a gathering of peace officers. He told me that he had never appeared before so many people who seemed to be so miserable.

Police work is conducted in an extremely negative environment. Tickets, arrests, serious injuries, and seeing death up close can cause a hardening of the heart and a negative attitude. This environment does not lend itself well to effective policing or a happy life.

Many people in protest movements, especially those on the far left, have fallen into a similar psychological morass of cynicism and unhappiness. Many of them are violent, hateful, and miserable. They ignore the freedom and opportunity they have that could be used for doing something good.

When one lives in the negativity of these two worlds, it is difficult to have hope and to believe that there is a God who loves you.

Billy Graham said he believed that if any person sincerely turns to the Lord, God will reveal himself. Jesus promises in Revelation 3:20: "Behold, I stand at the door and knock; If anyone hears my voice and opens the door I will come in to him, and will dine with him and he with me." (NASB)

While it's difficult for peace officers and many protesters to believe in God, it seems that those who have a real and abiding relationship with Jesus behave far better and cope well with the perils that these tragedies present.

6) Avoid high-risk situations at all costs

The number of people killed in police incidents each year is about 1000. Most of those killed are involved in high risk situations including shootouts, running from the police, assaulting the police, brandishing weapons, taking away an officer's gun, and resisting arrest. Many people killed are also under the influence of alcohol or drugs.

The percentages of those killed are roughly the same for all races involved in the same types of incidents and exhibiting similar behaviors.

In fact, when comparing similar cases and high-risk behavior, whites were slightly more likely to be killed than blacks. African American officers were slightly more likely to use deadly force against black suspects than white officers in similar situations.

No matter how inconvenient these facts may be, we must address them to isolate and address true prejudice and to save lives.

The best advice to avoid getting injured or killed is to comply with officer commands, never run from the police especially at night, never resist arrest or get in a struggle with peace officers. Those of any race who do are exposing themselves to a high-risk situation.

"Discretion will guard you, Understanding will watch over you, …" Proverbs 2:11 (NASB)

7) Reject meritless kneejerk solutions

Protests of George Floyd's death expanded into full scale progressive revolts in Portland and Seattle. Cities across the country suffered billions of dollars of damage from so-called "mostly peaceful protests." The police had been ordered to stand down while murders and violent assaults had risen precipitously. Nonetheless, loud voices demanded eliminating or defunding the police.

Sometimes the loudest voices are the most stupid. Some of the radical changes proposed were already in force and responsible for the deaths of far more people of color than those who die in incidents involving the police.

Weak, ineffectual leadership in several big cities accomplished the unimaginable. In addition to all the deaths and injuries, tens of thousands of businesses and livelihoods were destroyed, *causing even more moderate individuals to buy guns and assault weapons in record numbers with sales reaching nearly 4 million in June, 2020.*
FBI Says It Conducted A Record-High 3.9 Million Gun ... - NPR
www.npr.org› sections › 2020/07/02 › amid-virus-fears-

Defunding the police was a really bad idea and certainly qualified as a meritless kneejerk reaction.

"Wise men store up knowledge, but with the mouth of the foolish, ruin is at hand." Proverbs 10:14 (NASB)

8) Reject violent, hateful, discredited ideologies

Communism and Socialism have been vessels of tyranny, revolution, and misery for a hundred years. These two ideologies have robbed people of their freedom and basic rights, are ruled by immoral tyrants, and responsible for the killing of tens of millions of people.

These systems are so bereft of decency that the bulk of the millions murdered were their own citizens, killed for political expedience.

The rights of the state become sacrosanct and individual rights are so far diminished that "No Lives Matter." Ronald Reagan was never more correct than when he proclaimed these systems would wind up in the ash heap of history.
Ash heap of history - Wikipedia
en.wikipedia.org› wiki › Ash_heap_of_history

It's hard to imagine that in America today so many seemingly sane, intelligent people fail to recognize the inherent folly of such a thoroughly discredited form of government. It's equally disappointing to see elected leaders sworn to defend the Constitution allow or tacitly encourage violent mobs who are ruining American cities with tactics that would make Mussolini smile.

"...The foundations of law and order have collapsed. What can the righteous do?" Psalm 11:3 (NLT)

9) Reject false narratives and misinformation

For many years, peace officers have bought into a medical myth that can have deadly results.

There is a mistaken belief that if someone is able to talk, they are breathing sufficiently and not in danger of passing out or even worse.

This false belief undoubtedly played a part in the deaths of Eric Garner (July 17, 2014) and George Floyd. Both clearly warned officers verbally that they were having trouble breathing.

Had the officers paid better attention and recognized sooner that these incidents had become medical emergencies, it is possible that neither man would have died.

When acted upon misinformation, false narratives can have profoundly negative results.

Many politicians, media members, and protestors have bought into a popular but false narrative. Most of what they believe about systemic racism is false.

Systemic racism is not the reason higher numbers of minorities are in prison. Committing violent crimes is far more causative. The introduction of violence into one's criminal behavior is the number one reason people go to prison.

Thousands of years of prison time has little to do with race, and everything to do with rape, robbery, murder, and aggravated assault.

Any group or sub group of society that commits violent crimes in greater numbers, will have a higher percentage of people in prison and jail.

Most of the elements that are characterized as systematic racism are more correctly understood as disadvantages that all people who are poor experience in the criminal justice system.

Being poor and a person of color can be a disadvantage as to whether one beats a few of the cases along the way. Having a legal dream team helped O.J. Simpson and Robert Blake beat murder raps.

O. J. Simpson murder case - Wikipedia
en.wikipedia.org› wiki › O._J._Simpson_murder_case
Actor Robert Blake acquitted of wife's murder - HISTORY
www.history.com› this-day-in-history › robert-blake

Very few poor people are able to beat the system.

"The righteous is concerned for the rights of the poor, The wicked do not understand such concern."
Proverbs 29:7 (NASB)

10) Accept inconvenient truths and make appropriate changes

Police officers work in a negative environment often dealing with people at their worst. Many officers become bitter, callous, and lose their ability to empathize.

Peace officers need to get regular heart level training to help counter negative hardened attitudes.

Deadly force permanently alters life and communities. Many incidents unfold quickly and in ways where there are few alternatives, and no good choices.

Officers need regular training and better force alternatives if we are going to hold them accountable by firing and prosecuting them for split-second decisions made in tense rapidly evolving circumstances. More research and development are needed to find less offensive force options that help officers subdue suspects before situations devolve into deadly force incidents.

African Americans, though composing only about 15% of the population, commit roughly half of all murders and a disproportionately high number of robberies and assaults. These are the violent crimes most likely to result in incarceration and cause the extra police attention, and more of the situations that result in the use of deadly force.

We must address underlying cultural, economic, and social causes of high crime. We need more programs and the social will to keep nuclear families together. Economic opportunity zones, better security for public housing, and locating magnet schools with highly sought-after programs in depressed areas, might also help families and improve communities.

"In everything, therefore, treat people the same way you want them to treat you, for this is the Law of the Prophets." Matthew 7:12 (NASB)

Victory over Injustice

Throughout our history great men and woman have lived, fought, and died for the cause of justice. Anything that robs our citizens of their right to life, liberty, and the pursuit of happiness—is injustice.

America is under attack as never before. In addition to the tragic death of George Floyd, violence and unrest in the streets have created new victims and ruined communities.

Perhaps most insidious is that while racism and prejudice are universally condemned, so many fail to recognize hateful violent protests for what they are—injustice.

In light of all the trauma, what is our best hope for achieving justice for our citizens? How can we overcome the racism, prejudice, and crime that plague us?

At the core of injustice are basic human immoralities (sin) and we can only overcome them with a change of heart.

Jesus changes hearts. Turning to Him, asking Him to come into your life as Lord and Savior is the best hope to overcome the selfishness, hatred, and bitterness that afflict us all.

Jesus changes hearts.

The love and forgiveness that Jesus gives provides the best chance to end the violence, and stop the last vestiges of racism, prejudice, and crime. Only then will we truly fulfill the promises of freedom and liberty for all of our citizens, and safeguard the American Dream for future generations. Only then will we be a "Just Nation."

Matthew 11:28-29 (NASB) **28** "Come to Me, all who are weary and heavy-laden, and I will give you rest. **29** Take My yoke upon you and learn from Me, for I am gentle and humble in heart, and you will find rest for your souls."

*****

Author's Note: **Larry Wolf** and I originally became acquainted 30+ years ago, when he was working as a coach for a local gym, and I was honored to have him as my coach! He is a gifted writer of music and plays, and we have been honored to publish two of his books through Creative Team Publishing. In fact, he is writing a third book. As a career, he serves as the Department Chair of Criminal Justice at the University of Antelope Valley in Lancaster, California. Larry is a Christian and possesses and lives a vibrant testimony. And he is great friend. He is an effective speaker and presents truth from a heart of honesty.

Chapter 14
Through Extreme Pain and Loss, God Helps Us Endure

Lenny and Grace Belvedere
Owners of Ottavio's Restaurant, Lakeside, California

August 19, 2020

[Author: Recounted here is the painful loss of the children of Lenny and Grace Belvedere to a lone gunman at Christmastime in 2013. The details are sad, graphic, and pointed. Often Lenny and Grace have questioned: "Where is God? Where was God in all of this?" You may ask, "How has survival beyond tragedy even been possible?" The crises of the murders of three precious, young family members are presented to reveal this everlasting truth: out of our greatest losses and through our deepest pains, hope can arise. The God of all comfort is present; He is here. You can trust Him.]

Lenny:

I met Glen Aubrey back in 1999. He often came to our restaurant which was in El Cajon, California at the time. He would set up a writing corner in the back (in an annex), and work while he ate.

His favorite menu item was then and remains today: Chopped Chicken Salad, fresh Focaccia Bread, Soup (on Fridays) and Cabernet Sauvignon. We got to know each other well starting then, and now lasting for over twenty years.

Anyone who knows me also knows I'm a very private person. I will disclose only on a need-to-know basis; however, by the request of my dear friend Glen, I will share with you from the depths of my soul what is extremely painful; it's nearly impossible to relate the indescribable.

My wife and I had been married for 38 years. We raised five children together, three girls and two boys, into adulthood. Gianni and Salvatore were the youngest. They were adored by their sister, brother-in laws, nieces, and nephews. My sons were the life of the party. Both where musically gifted and worked hard to develop their skills at a young age. Gianni was a pianist and Sal played the guitar. They were not only talented, but Sal was always there lending a shoulder to cry on and he had a heart of gold. Gianni was charismatic, funny, and inspired others; he was highly respected by the public and his peers. Ask one who knew them, and they would tell you the same things.

Our children were raised on a Catholic foundation. We instilled values that were essential to our family and necessary for the children to become contributing adults who were self-disciplined, compassionate, and responsible.

Just like many families we had our problems, of course; we were not a perfect family but at the end of the day we always worked out whatever problems we had.

The two younger boys were in their early 20s in 2013, and were just becoming men. They had grown up in a third-generation family restaurant. I felt confident leaving this legacy of the restaurant to my sons and daughters. I figured that in my retirement years I could rest assured that all my children would have a strong family bond and they could make it through life together.

As a business owner I have weathered many financial crises, but I never could have imagined how one crucial instant in time could bring me and my family eternal suffering and damage for the remainder of our lives.

Christmas Eve morning of 2013, my life ended with a knock at the door and two police saying, "Your son has been shot and is clinging to life; he's on life support, but your daughter-in-law was pronounced deceased with a gunshot through the head." Both of them had been murdered in their car in cold blood. My eldest son was pronounced deceased later; he was shot in his car after a search for him lasting two weeks.

That seemed impossible! The night before had been a late night; we were preparing for a grand opening of our new restaurant. I had said goodnight. The last words I never will forget were: "Goodnight, dad; ... 'see you in the morning."

The unimaginable was real! The murderer was still at large and there were no witnesses.

In the days and weeks following their deaths, I was forced to prepare for three funerals and memorial services. I had to deal with the media, the police, the legal system, and a host of other stressful anxieties. There was no psychologist on earth that could fix this; they could only teach you how to live with it for the rest of your life. It's like drowning a slow, agonizing death.

Prayers from close family and friends; even strangers supported us. Everyone needed answers.

Finally, there was a break; our prayers were starting to be answered: the murderer was identified and arrested.

By Divine intervention he was picked up at a random early morning border patrol checkpoint. They discovered rifles, a semi-automatic handgun, and automatic weapons that were visible in the back seat of his car. When asked, he said he was going to Hollywood, in Los Angeles.

He was an incompetent, unbalanced, and deranged individual who had no motive calling himself an assassin.

Movies of killings, guns, and violence were found in his computer.

There was no motive or reason for him to kill our children. After two years of pleading insanity, and to avoid the death penalty, he finally pleaded guilty to all three murders with no explanation of why he had committed these heinous acts. He is serving three consecutive life sentences with no possibility of parole.

My wife and I asked ourselves every day, "How could this have happened?" "Where was God and why all three children?" I felt betrayed by God; I had lost not one, or two, but three children under one roof.

Since 2013, there has been increased madness of gun violence. It is now believable that it's not uncommon for someone to kill without an intentional motive.

I never imagined I'd still be here today. If it weren't for my wife, my daughters, and grandchildren, I don't know how I would have ended up.

My wife constantly tells me to look at the countless lives our children had touched before and after death. There were so many!

My youngest son clung to life; he was on life support for three days after being shot. We had to make the horrible decision to take him off the ventilator when he was declared brain dead. We never knew he had a rare blood type. His license was checked off to be a donor if anything was to happen to him.

A nurse approached us telling us that his rare blood type would save many people. His heart, kidneys, and liver now have saved three lives by the gifting of his own.

Police believed it was a miracle that the murderer was stopped at the checkpoint. They believed with all the guns in his backseat that he was on his way for another mass shooting.

The police department, detective, attorneys, and teams who worked on this case never stopped talking about what an honor it was to take the case; that it was their true privilege getting to know our incredible family and the strength and courage they saw; they had never seen anything like it before. Our story changed their lives forever.

Countless strangers have approached our families giving condolences and have said, "You have touched our lives. We couldn't imagine what you are going through ... it makes our hardships seem easier and we have a greater appreciation and gratitude for what we are given in our family."

Maybe if it were not for tragic events we would not learn and show our compassion. Take an Amber Alert as an example—out of a horrible event, lessons are learned, and many lives can be saved.

I may appear strong to others, but I would often like to crawl into a corner and never face the world again. But what options are there? Should we lie down, give up, and let the darkness overcome us, or should we be responsible, aware, and take care of our families? The choice for us is clear. We must and will be responsible, renewed, and strong through God's power.

In the end, there is no authority to which to turn for truth as to the reason why this horrible event occurred, no system that can fix this tragic event. In the end there is just acceptance and determination. I have an obligation to my sons. *Yes*, I can hear the whispers in my soul and to my conscience from my sons: "Don't give up, Dad; stay strong. Mom and the girls need you. You'll be with us soon enough, Dad. Know that we are at peace."

I know that there are wonderful, honest, truly loving people in the world because I see them all the time. I also know that our thoughts and feelings are very powerful, and when we are led down a path of darkness, it is sometimes very hard to see the light.

My wife tells me she knows that my sons and daughter-in-law left this earth by offering their lives so that at least one person may learn something. They did not die in vain.

I constantly remind myself: "There is only LOVE where my sons reside."

I now have a different relationship with the Spirit of God. *Rather than looking for faith in times of uncertainty or tribulation, I live with the help of my son's spirits and memories to guide me in this world so I can be reunited with them in another place after my death, in the divine presence of God.*

As a business owner I constantly interact with customers, every day. Things had gotten very chaotic in 2020, very complicated in the whole world as we knew it. Regardless, I try to keep my private struggles private ... that my crosses don't become burdens to others while trying to give reassurance to others.

My wife tells me she knows that my sons and daughter-in-law left this earth by offering their lives so that at least one person may learn something. They did not die in vain. I constantly remind myself: "There is only LOVE where my sons reside."

*****

Grace (From her Homily):

I have been inspired to share with you as a mother about the loss of our children. For those of you who have children and never experienced this loss, you could only imagine.

I'm sure you are all asking yourselves, "How do you continue on with life?" I can tell you this ... you can never prepare.

Since I was 33 years old, I have been battling an illness. I call it the invisible illness, and doctors called it M.E. It changed my life dramatically. No longer could I stand on my feet. I've had no strength to cook a meal, attend to my children's needs, or lead a normal life as a wife and mother.

Most of us look at illness as a horrible time in our lives, a time of suffering and pain. I understand why we feel this way. I struggled with the inability to get out of bed from weakness and pain. The kids really don't remember a time when I wasn't sick. My children spent a lot of time hanging out in my bedroom while I was in bed. We snuggled. They cheered me up. We talked, giggled, and cried together.

My children and husband made a lot of sacrifices, and somehow managed to do things on their own. As the years passed, they worked together as a team and we got through it. If you asked me in the beginning of my illness, I would have said, "I was miserable and mad at God. What did I do to deserve this?" I would beg Him to cure me. Why would He not restore my health? I desperately wanted to be a normal mother and wife.

Somewhere in the middle of it, I realized there are only two paths I could choose. I could stop believing there was a God. Hate Him and never pray again.

Which is the easy way out? Accept this cross and bear it … which is the hardest road. So, I chose to take the hard road.

My illness over the years has opened me to gratitude — the desire to appreciate life fully and to see what I have that's right in front of me. I learned that I was way more than my physical shell. That my soul, my spirit, was a real part of me. The only one there for me, still loving me, ever constant and always reliable, has been God. So, I've got to know Him better. It seemed the right thing to do.

My prayer life is now very active. It definitely has brought me closer to God. For one thing it has helped me to think of God more in everyday life. It has also helped me to let go of the trivial things in the material world that have distracted me from my relationship with God.

Gradually, I came to accept the idea that perhaps I never could go back to my old life. I can get by and be satisfied with so much less than I did before. I learned that death was no longer my biggest fear … living was.

I learned that death was no longer my biggest fear ... living was.

Now, three of my beloved children have been taken away. I've been asking the Lord every day, "Why did you let this tragedy happen to our families? Why didn't You step in and save protect our loved ones? I have known of angels intervening and warning people from tragedy. Why didn't that happen with Gianni, Ilona and Sal?"

"Why, Lord? We are good parents, we prayed, and we taught them good morals. There has never been any violence in our families. Why lord? Are we being punished? We were a happy family; we were good parents; why disrupt our happy life? What did we do to deserve this?"

So here I am again asking God, "Why did You take these three precious children from me? How much more suffering can I endure once again?" I find myself at that crossroad again. Do I choose to hate God? Or finish my life with prayer, courage, and endure the rest of my life without my sons and Ilona? If God is infinitely good, why does He allow so much evil and suffering in the world?

Although I don't think God causes evil, He does allow evil to be done by creatures who possess a free will. There are people who willingly choose to live in the hellish nightmare of hatred and uncontrolled, murderous jealousy. God gave people freedom of choice, and while He allows people to choose to do evil, could God arrange a coincidental miracle to counteract the intended evil? How many evil deeds *does* He stop, and we simply don't know about His intervention?

Prayer alone does not always stop evil—Satan is powerful and has great influence in this world today. Prayer alone cannot stop every tragedy. However, prayer—intimate conversation with God—can help us understand and cope with tragedies like this. And I hear the words of St. Thomas Aquinas, "Two things happen when there is a tragedy: God permits evil in order to draw forth some greater good, and maybe it could prevent a greater evil." I already see a greater good; my younger son, Sal, gave the gift of life, He gave his precious heart on Christmas to another person so they may live. He also saved two other lives with the organs he donated.

So, here lies my growing sadness and sorrow. I'm supposed to die before my young sons. "Why didn't You take me? How, Lord, could you leave me here to endure this suffering? Should I seek revenge on the people that did this to my family?"

Justice? Yes! Revenge? No. No, because the anger and hatred would imprison me, and I would be consumed with hatred in my heart.

But once again I will take up my cross and sorrow and continue to walk with Jesus in his footsteps on the road to Calvary. "I'm not alone," I tell myself ... "Jesus is by my side." At the end of my earthly journey, my precious handsome sons will be there with open arms to receive me. Then I can live in peace without fear, without separation, without wanting and suffering. No more fears, no more tears; just pure unconditional love and eternal happiness.

So, pray, forgive. Give lots of hugs. Call or send a text to your loved ones. Tell them you love them unconditionally because tomorrow they may not be there. Help support the control on guns, so they don't end up in the wrong hands. Don't let revenge and hatred fester in your hearts. But forgive and love unconditionally and walk with the Lord to the end.

Forgive and love unconditionally and walk with the Lord to the end.

Our families would like to extend our gratitude for all your prayers and support that you have given us through this horrible tragedy. But please continue praying for us to have the courage and strength to go on with our lives.

Lenny and Grace Belvedere, "Through Extreme Pain and Loss, God Helps Us Endure"

*****

Author's Note: From the opening of this chapter: "Out of our greatest losses and through our deepest pains, hope can arise. The God of all comfort is present; He is here. You can trust Him." The hearts of two precious people are revealed in this chapter. I want to personally thank both **Lenny and Grace Belvedere** for their contributions to this book. They inspire all who know them and their stories, to trust God more fully, in every crisis and challenge. Lenny and Grace are renewed in times of crises as you and I can be as well. Take encouragement from them, and then encourage others who face difficult moments that can last a very long time.

Chapter 15
When Important Things Fail

Mike Atkinson, Owner/Publisher of Mikey's Funnies
www.MikeysFunnies.com

August 30, 2020

"I've scheduled your emergency biopsy for this Monday."

My head was swirling. I received this call out of nowhere from someone called a nephrologist. He told me I had kidney problems and we needed to diagnose it right away. The next few weeks were filled with so much new and concerning information. It was like drinking water from a fire hydrant.

A nephrologist is a kidney doctor and he told me I had an autoimmune disease that had been eating away the filters on my kidneys over time. I found out that I would go through intensive therapies with strong medications and infusions (with a long list of side effects) to hopefully reverse this process.

When the treatment didn't work, my kidneys rapidly degraded into failure, which led to dialysis. Then the T-word was spoken—transplant.

I went through all kinds of emotions. How did I get here? What happened to my "normal" life? Would I survive this? I realized I didn't appreciate good health until I lost it.

A bevy of medical tests was next for me to qualify for a kidney transplant. I passed. I got the word out to family and friends about the need for a transplant. I ended up with 20 people who offered to donate their kidney. I was overwhelmed with this beautiful, deeply kind gesture. Ultimately, a young family friend was chosen, not because she was a match for me, but because of her blood type, she would be a potential match for others having problems finding a donor.

That put us in the Paired Donor Exchange Program. They quickly found a match for my donor with a woman who was not doing well because she was hard to match. And they found a donor for me quickly. A date was set.

On December 29, 2015, all three of us went into the hospital. My original donor was first, taking out her kidney and flying it to the recipient in another state. Then my direct donor was taken into the OR, where doctors took out his kidney, and tested it. All was well, so I went in and they transplanted it into my body. My recovery was long, but at least I was vertical (most days).

There were some immediate blessings from this experience. Later, I was blessed to officiate the wedding of my original donor. Standing in front of the person who helped save my life, in a beautiful wedding gown, smiling from ear to ear, is an image that will never leave my memory. A very special day.

Another blessing from this experience was a new friendship with my direct donor. He and I are very similar and get along great. He ultimately moved to the same city as me and we all enjoy spending time together.

He and I love to tell this story from just after the transplant. In the hospital, his caretaker came up to see how I was doing and we connected on Facebook. When she left, I started looking at her profile and noticed that my direct donor had posted an update after surgery. He said that he got to meet me right before the transplant surgery—a very strange turn of events—and that I was wearing a beanie that said BLESSED and my pastor was with my wife, Stacy, and me. His response was, "I didn't have the heart to tell him that he was getting an atheist kidney." I laughed heartily and replied, "Atheist no more." That was the beginning of a special friendship.

From the Physical to the Spiritual

While there I experienced an incredible amount of physical changes—aches, pains, transformations during those short two years—there were far more spiritual changes that continued in the ensuing years.

After a very hard day at work—a lot of stress on top of having a rough day healthwise—I got in my car. I was down, way down. Just then my phone rang. It was my pastor. He allowed me to unload on him, which helped. At the end of our conversation, he said, "Sounds like the makings of a good sermon." We chuckled.

But that statement stuck with me. A year and a half later, I delivered that sermon, and he was right. I had plenty of material from the past few years. I had learned much about my Heavenly Father and myself. That sermon is the basis of what I share with you here.

God Is Still...Present

I learned much about the presence of God through those years. From what I read in the Bible, He does not promise rosy days of easy living. He *does* promise to be with us—guiding us, loving us, forgiving us, offering His wisdom. That became so real for me.

It became very real in one tangible way. Dialysis was not easy. It affected me. But, in my case, it kept me alive until the transplant, the ultimate purpose of dialysis. Every night I would connect a tube coming from my abdomen to the dialysis machine that would run all night pumping in fluid that would absorb the bad stuff and then flush them out another tube. That may seem gross to you, but it was life-giving for me.

I had to set my mind on that goal of dialysis, to stay alive. I couldn't focus on the negative aspects of the process. So, each time I connected the tube, I prayed that God would actually be in the solution pumping into my body; that His will would be done that night.

Albert Einstein said, "Adversity introduces a man to himself."[1] Boy, was that true for me. It showed me what I was made of. And sometimes it wasn't pretty. I had a lot of dark days, and there were times I got mean and nasty. Unfortunately, my wife, Stacy, was usually the recipient of the ugliness. It took a toll on her, as it does most caregivers. And since my transplant, if I get whiney or down, she just looks at me and says, "At least you're not on dialysis." She's always had a way of bringing me back to a realistic perspective.

[1] www.goodreads.com

In these years, I learned to rely on my faith however it looked at that moment. When faced with adversity, *all* you have is the faith you have at that moment. Start there. Don't focus on what your faith isn't—deep, constant, amazing. Focus on what it is: maybe weak, shaky, confused. It's all you have, and God embraces you as you are, providing exactly what you need to persevere.

"He doesn't exult in your pain, but He delights in your tighter embrace."

~ David Jeremiah "A Bend in the Road: Finding God When Your World Caves In"

All this led me to realize that I needed to accept the reality, but hope for the divine. The reality was that my kidneys were failing. I may or may not survive this. But no amount of worrying, anxiety, or crying would change my situation. It is what it is.

> ...accept the reality, but hope for the divine.

I had a hope in God, a confidence in His unconditional love. I can anticipate God to be present in the struggle—guiding me, leading the way.

I come from a long line of nuclear-strength worriers. I knew I had to curtail that natural inclination in order to survive this. In church one day in 2016 I wrote this:

Easy.

By Mike Atkinson

O Lord, how can I fret when you walk with me?

Easy.

My mind is small, confined, tunnel-visioned.
The things of Earth grow strangely bright,
instead of dim. I envy the lilies, which toil
not. [Hard to imagine a toil-free existence.]
Worry is threaded through my DNA. Trying
to remember a point in life when worries
added a single moment to my life.
Easy.
They didn't. And yet I cling to it, like an
addict. Just one more hit ... like it does me
any good. Solomon said, "So refuse to worry,
and keep your body healthy." Sounds like a
relevant goal. Jesus said, "That is why I tell
you not to worry about everyday life.
Today's trouble is enough for today." So,
today. Today I will choose to breathe
surrender. A daily—no hourly; nay,
minutely—decision.
Things above over things below. Yes to
St. Paul, who said, "Don't worry about
anything ... tell God what you need, and thank
Him for all He has done." Thank You, Father.

Don't sweat what you can't control. Worry is toxic and leads to anger and bitterness. Choose to be better, not bitter. I couldn't control getting this illness. The autoimmune disease

I had was random, striking children, marathon runners, the elderly; people from every walk got it.

"Suffering was, is, and will be a part of life here on earth. Lean into suffering as best you can. Don't blame God, connect with Him. He'll go through it with you. And that is enough."
~ Regi Campbell Radical Mentoring website, "Suffering Sucks" https://radicalmentoring.com/suffering-sucks/

We have a lot of ravens in our neighborhood. They are large, imposing, black figures in the sky. But these little, annoying mockingbirds constantly squawk and dive-bomb these large birds, many times digging their claws into their backs. It happens while they're flying, but it also happens when they're sitting on a phone or power line. They're persistently bombarded by these winged irritations, and they don't do anything about it. I'm sure when they were young, they thought they could. But as they got older, they realized they would never catch one of those nimble mockingbirds. So, they sit there and accept it—still exasperating, but why let it ruin your day?

"Consider the ravens: They do not sow or reap, they have no storeroom or barn; yet God feeds them. And how much more valuable you are than birds!"
~ Jesus, Luke 12:24

Acceptance is not an easy-to-reach destination. Certainly, there is room for intervention and even miracles. But the health of our mind, of our spirit, is based on our mindset. If we consistently dwell on the things we cannot control, we can do damage to our health—mental and physical—and our relationships.

"Occasionally weep deeply over the life you hoped would be. Grieve the losses. Then wash your face. Trust God. And embrace the life you have."
~ John Piper, Twitter, March 1, 2016

So many times I experience the presence of God through His children. It was Easter morning, during the time I was starting dialysis. My kidneys had failed and I was weak. When friends had seen me, they commented to Stacy about their concern for my pale, grey complexion. I felt horrible but forced myself to go to church on this special day on the church calendar.

I sat in my chair during the service praying for resurrection, hoping for resurrection. At that point, my phone vibrated. Now, any good Christian wouldn't check their phone in church. So, I checked my phone. It was a text from a good friend who was in Israel at the time. He said he was at the Wailing Wall and had asked their guide to write my name in Hebrew on a piece of paper. He then approached the Wall and, like so many pilgrims, placed the paper in a crack in the

Wall and prayed for me. I quietly sobbed in my chair, realizing that God has truly answered my prayer.

"Michael" in Hebrew, inserted into the Wailing Wall:

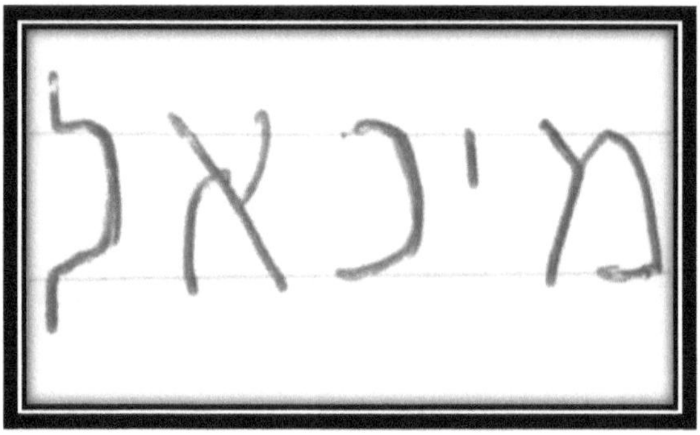

God Is Still...On The Throne

"God is good all the time" ... "All the time God is good."

How many of us have participated in this call-and-response? There's something powerful in a group of people affirming this truth together with raised voices.

But through my struggles, I had to ask myself if I truly owned that.

This phrase is a simple yet powerful truth. No matter what happens in your life, God is good. Period. Major disasters happen, people die, people lose homes, jobs, but God is still good. Remember that He relinquished His control of earth at the beginning when bad choices were made. So we suffer from wrong choices, bad consequences, illnesses, destructive lifestyles—and yet He is there, on the throne, ready to join me in my journey.

We're familiar with Shadrach, Meshach, and Abednego and the fiery furnace, but a lot of times we forget what led up to it. King Nebuchadnezzar had set up a gold statue for everyone to bow down and worship. But these three devout Jews would not kneel. They were brought to the King who had promised that anyone who didn't kneel would be thrown into the furnace. So he asked them, "Do you think there is any god who can save you?" They answered:

> "O Nebuchadnezzar, we do not need to defend ourselves before you. If we are thrown into the blazing furnace, the God whom we serve is able to save us. He will rescue us from your power, Your Majesty. ***But even if he doesn't,*** we want to make it clear to you, Your Majesty, that we will never serve your gods or worship the gold statue you have set up."
>
> Daniel 3:16-20 (emphasis mine) (NLT)
>
>

Even if He doesn't...

In my opinion, those four words are some of the most powerful in the Bible. We can hope for the divine. Pray for God's intervention. But *if He doesn't,* He is still good. He is still on the throne. He is still God. He doesn't promise to fix everything. He promises to walk this life with you and offer you His power to get through whatever may come.

There was one spiritual discipline I learned early on in this experience. Every night when my head hit the pillow, I thanked God for that day. Every single day. No matter what happened. No matter how dark or painful the day was or how much I dreaded the night. I did it. Sometimes through clenched teeth. And many times, I didn't mean it, but I forced myself to say it anyway.

Talk about an attitude adjustment. It forced me to return to the truth that even though everything that day may have sucked, I was still a blessed man. Blessed with a good life compared to most people on this planet; I was blessed with an angel wife, incredible children and even better grandchildren (wink), awesome family, and a great cloud of witnesses across the globe covering me in love, support, and prayer.

One day I happened to see this headline: "Thankfulness Protects Against PTSD." (Posttraumatic Stress Disorder) I was interested because some therapist friends said they saw evidence of PTSD in Stacy and me during and after this journey. The article covered a study of students at a university who were on campus when a shooting occurred.

Here's an excerpt of what they discovered:

> "Gratitude, of course, will not be our first response to trauma. It's impossible not to go through pain, confusion and anger when you hear about these tragedies, and even more so if you experience it firsthand. This response is called Post-Traumatic Stress (PTS), but there is also a second psychological concept called Post-Traumatic Growth (PTG). PTG happens in the season after the trauma, when some people start to feel thankful to be alive, thankful that the trauma wasn't even worse, and grateful for the chance to learn more about themselves.
>
> The results of the study showed that the individuals who already had higher levels of gratitude before the shooting were better able to turn their post-traumatic stress into growth. This is actually quite profound.

It suggests that if we can help ourselves and others feel more grateful on a daily basis, we can actually prime ourselves to handle the trauma that life will inevitably bring."
(https://www.christianitytoday.com/ct/2017/july-web-only/thankfulness-protects-against-ptsd.html)

Part of the study asked one group of students to make a list at the end of their day of everything they were thankful for—an hour with their best friend, passing a test, gestures of kindness, moments of natural beauty—stuff they may not even recognize as things they should be grateful for. The other group was asked to list everything that frustrated or angered them that day. Not surprisingly, the first group reported feeling healthier, having a more positive mood, exercising more, and feeling better about their lives in general.

I found that many times through this illness I retreated into myself—getting too self-focused. It's very easy to do with a chronic illness. But I don't read anywhere in the Bible that people with chronic illness get a pass on serving others. No asterisk, no disclaimer, no exceptions. Still a command.

"If your spiritual practice doesn't lead you to some acts of concrete caring or service then you have every reason not to trust it ... We can only give who we are. We can only offer to others what God has done in us."
~ Fr. Richard Rohr, OFM, "Contemplation in Action"

When I was diagnosed and got a sense of the seriousness of the situation, we decided not to let this disease define us. We refused to give it that kind of power in our lives. For us, that meant a campaign to spread joy to whoever God put in our path.

... we decided not to let this disease define us.
We refused to give it that kind of power in our lives.
For us, that meant a campaign to spread joy to whoever God put in our path.

That meant loving on those who cared for me—doctors, surgeons, nurses, physician's assistants, lab techs, imaging specialists, pharmacists, you name it. Stacy was so good about caring for them. I could usually make them laugh. We wanted them to feel valued and appreciated.

My dialysis nurse, Joanie, was an angel, patiently teaching me and walking me through the whole process. After my transplant, there was one task I couldn't wait to perform. I wanted to return to my dialysis center. I knew I had to return to thank her and the other nurses who also helped. So, we did one afternoon after a follow-up appointment with my surgeon. There were a lot of hugs and tears with all of them. We brought them cookies and flowers—believe me, *very* small tokens. We hugged them and thanked them for helping us back to life, and we reminded them of how important their holy mission is.

This is the kind of difference we can make by getting outside of ourselves and our circumstances to be the hands and feet of Jesus.

Now I try to watch for people in my vicinity each day who may need support or affirmation. That awareness is not easy to develop, and I still struggle with it. It takes a while for it to be part of our daily muscle memory.

"I want a lifetime of holy moments. Every day I want to be in dangerous proximity to Jesus. I long for a life that explodes with meaning and is filled with adventure, wonder, risk, and danger. I long for a faith that is gloriously treacherous. I want to be with Jesus, not knowing whether to cry or laugh."
~ Mike Yaconelli, www.mikeyaconelli.org

God Is Still...Crazy In Love With Me

"Jesus comes not for the super-spiritual but for the wobbly and the weak-kneed who know they don't have it all together, and who are not too proud to accept the handout of amazing grace."
~Brennan Manning "The Ragamuffin Gospel"

All the wobbly out there, can I get an Amen?

I have always gravitated to God as Father. You see I grew up without a father. I was born out of wedlock from an affair. As a result, my strong and amazing mother moved to San Diego to get help from her family. As an aside: I didn't meet my father until I was 19 and he became one of the most important people in my life.

But before that, I was fatherless. I was introduced to Jesus in 7th grade at an after-school Bible Club. I immediately absorbed this big, monumental story of salvation and redemption. I found that I leaned on God, the Father, often, as I may have leaned on an earthly father.

Then I became a father—boy, did I become a father! Eight kids later and I didn't even have a father figure to emulate. When we were newly married, I knew we would have children so I started watching fathers closely to see how they did the father thing. I prayed, a lot, because it was unfamiliar territory for me. I depended heavily on the modeling of God the Father in scripture.

Unfortunately, for way too many people, this idea of God the Father is not a comforting one, because of their father. So many broken men breaking their children. So many of my friends growing up in abusive homes, or with irresponsible fathers or absent fathers. I understand how this is a huge hurdle for folks.

I found that I could submit to my heavenly Father because He is the perfect father Who makes up for any and all failings of every human father in history. He is all-powerful and all-knowing and yet He loves us anyway—and not just loves us, but loves us without condition. There is *nothing* you can do to make Him stop loving you. Let me just pause on that to let it sink in.

I repeat: NOTHING.

He has a plan for you, which involves much more about *who you are* than what you do or have. He's a Healer, bringing us through a process of facing and dealing with our baggage so we can become a lover of others. He's a Guide when we lose our way. He extends mercy when we least deserve it.

No earthly father can do all that as perfectly as God—just ask any of my kids.

"The grace of God is dangerous. It's lavish, excessive, outrageous, and scandalous. God's grace is ridiculously inclusive. Apparently, God doesn't care who He loves. He is not very careful about the people He calls His friends or the people He calls His church."
~ Mike Yaconelli, www.mikeyaconelli.org

I am *so* thankful that God is careless in the acceptance of his children—else I would not be here.

And now I invite you on this wild ride—be it coming into a relationship with God the Father, or wearing gratitude daily, or bringing the love of Jesus to those in your vicinity.

It's hard and not what we're naturally wired to do. It's just not easy, But man, what a ride!

> "You guide me with your counsel, leading me to a glorious destiny. Whom have I in heaven but you? I desire you more than anything on earth. My health may fail, and my spirit may grow weak, but God remains the strength of my heart; he is mine forever.
> Psalm 73:24-26 NLT

Mike Atkinson, "When Important Things Fail"

*****

Author's Note: **Mike Atkinson** is a longtime friend. He and I served Youth for Christ (YFC), San Diego, in the 80s. After YFC, he moved to Youth Specialties, a cutting-edge youth ministry enterprise. He developed the weekday email ***Mikey's Funnies***, a free resource to anyone who needs a clean humor lift: **www.MikeysFunnies.com**. He is a *gifted and creative thinker*. He is also a nationally recognized grower of plumerias; it's a passion. I recall when his kidney transplant was being planned. His recounting that story speaks of heart-felt commitment. He encourages others who face crises of unknown proportions. Mike and I remember: former employees of YFC were brought together for the memorial service for an employee of YFC who had been an anchor to the staff for years. Her name was Bobbi (Robertson) Underwood, a dear friend to YFC staff. I was privileged to play for her memorial service. Then, as my grandchildren came along (now eight), I shared original compositions, one written for each grandchild, with Mike and others, and he was always appreciative. He is a *giver and ministry builder*. He was a courageous leader, who served as Board of Directors President of YFC, San Diego. Through ***Mikey's Funnies*** he often places ads on behalf of our book authors. Mike, you are one of whom can be said, "Well done!"

Chapter 16
Be Strong and Courageous, Alive in Hope

Mark A. Chrysler, Electrical Inspection Consultant, San Diego Gas & Electric
Author
*Authentic Hope * Experiencing God's Presence When You Are an Unwilling Participant * "Living Life with a Footnote"*

September 16, 2020

Jesus taught us to love those who may oppose us, to bless and pray for those who may disagree, even express hatred toward us. In Matthew 5:43-48, a part of the Beatitudes, He stated specifically,

> 43 "You have heard that it was said, 'Love your neighbor and hate your enemy.' 44 But I tell you, love your enemies and pray for those who persecute you, 45 that you may be children of your Father in heaven. He causes his sun to rise on the evil and the good, and sends rain on the righteous and the unrighteous. 46 If you love those who love you, what reward will you get? Are not even the tax collectors doing that?

> 47 "And if you greet only your own people, what are you doing more than others? Do not even pagans do that? 48 Be perfect, therefore, as your heavenly Father is perfect."

I believe as a Christ follower the proverbial path to follow is found and described in the words penned by the Apostle Paul. He charges the believers to be diligent in the practice of their faith, regardless of difficulty or severity of crisis.

Remember what Jesus taught us? We are commanded to continue to live out our faith in *all* circumstances, no matter what they are. Paul warned that some people will follow teachers who are not advocating what Jesus taught while on this earth.

Paul gave instructions in a "charge" to his mentee, Timothy, recorded in 2 Timothy 4:1-4:

> "1 In the presence of God and of Christ Jesus, who will judge the living and the dead, and in view of his appearing and his kingdom, I give you this charge: 2 Preach the word; be prepared in season and out of season; correct, rebuke and encourage—with great patience and careful instruction. 3 For the time will come when people will not put up with sound doctrine. Instead, to suit their own desires, they will gather around them a great number of teachers

> to say what their itching ears want to hear.
> 4 They will turn their ears away from the truth
> and turn aside to myths."

The path I believe Jesus wants all those who trust Him to follow is narrow and may even be difficult at times to walk. Please see Matthew 7:13, 14:

> 13 "Enter through the narrow gate. For wide is the gate and broad is the road that leads to destruction, and many enter through it. 14 But small is the gate and narrow the road that leads to life, and only a few find it."

Jesus, while walking the earth, taught and preached and lived out God's plan for mankind. Please reference Mark 12:30-31. Jesus commanded us: "Love the Lord your God with all your heart, soul, mind, and strength," and "love your neighbor as yourself."

Love and hope rested in Paul's charge to Timothy, and in the Great Commandments of our Lord. In the final analysis, Jesus brought hope to mankind, authentic hope that transcends all circumstances.

This hope from God has a promise attached to it. When we trust Him and obey, God promises that in all circumstances, **He will never leave or forsake us.** (Hebrews 13:5)

If at times you feel alone, like the only one who is facing extremely difficult and even life-threatening crises for yourself or for others for whom you care, please be empowered by the words written by Moses thousands of years ago. These words teach us that when faced with adversity we can be strong and courageous.

Joshua 1:9 is a favorite passage of mine. It reads:

> 9 "Have I not commanded you? Be strong and courageous. Do not be afraid; do not be discouraged, for the LORD your God will be with you wherever you go."

Hope from God has a promise attached to it. When we trust Him and obey, God promises that in all circumstances, **He will never leave or forsake us.** (Hebrews 13:5)

*****

Author's Note: Mark Chrysler and I met through Youth for Christ (YFC), Campus Life, San Diego, in 1979. Events called "Breakaways," sponsored by YFC, were held at what was then known as the Point Loma College Bowl. These were extremely popular and well-attended outside, evening events with an average attendance of 1,500 high school kids. I was programming director and Mark was a spotlight operator, as he and I recalled. Mark had just become an Associate Director for Campus Life. Our friendship and cooperative ministry endeavors continued. Currently Mark graciously serves on my Board of Directors of Creative Ministry Teams, Inc. (CMT), a 501 (c) 3, a non-profit ministry, and he is now writing his first book, ***Authentic Hope * Experiencing God's Presence When You Are an Unwilling Participant * "Living Life with a Footnote"*** released in 2021. When he and his family were struggling with drug addiction of a family member as well as a personal cancer diagnosis (now in remission, thankfully), he and I would meet frequently in downtown La Mesa, California to share life and build one another up. We even consulted together in Washington, D.C. with the Department of Veteran's Affairs through Creative Team Resources Group (CTRG). His testimony and reliability have always proven true.

Chapter 17
Perspectives and Promises

September 17, 2020

When the creation of ***God's Plan Unfolding* * *Strength and Renewal in Times of Crisis*** was first considered, a select group of individuals was invited to be contributors to the work. It truly has been an honor nearly beyond measure to see what these individuals have willingly written. I am so grateful for their stories and perspectives.

Some contributors are old friends, others newer acquaintances. As you can readily see, these people represent a wide variety of ages, personal history, industries, interests, and vocations. In all cases a common thread was trust and reliance on God when facing the crises we all deal with, regardless of cause.

God is faithful. This truth binds the contributors together in theme and focus. Time and again throughout these true accounts you have witnessed firsthand, as I have, the complete and total reliance on God each individual expressed. My intention was not to assign specific topics or focus points; rather, to invite each participant to choose their own.

There was one proviso: I expressed to each writer that this book was to consist of true accounts of God's faithfulness. Collectively, we desired to see how God Who is unchanging, true, reliable, and worthy of our confidence, no matter the circumstance, sustained and lifted people who trusted Him and withstood their crises. We also wanted to see each contributor's response of faithfulness that was expressed as a commitment to remain committed, and to encourage others.

Several times in these writings you and I witnessed references to God's love, the overriding guiding and grounding principle of our faith. Love is God's character and His command for each of us to obey. Quotes about His love were not planned or "assigned" in consideration of the topics and contents chosen; they were freely contributed and formed a central and recurring theme throughout the book.

There is no stronger aspect to faith than God's unchanging love. Simply put, if we love God, we trust Him. There is no stronger solution and answer to life's crises than His love. We are told that perfect love casts out all fear. (1 John 4:18) That love is the central aspect of Godly character we choose because of His love shown to us. We are asked and commanded to emulate His love in all circumstances. This love endures through all time and in every crisis, period. It is a facet of Godly character we can employ and practice in any situation, anytime. It's our choice.

The perspectives you have read all come with a promise inherent in the faithfulness of God. It is this, in a brief summary for you: God promises to be with you, near you, and His presence will sustain you as you trust Him. This truth may be simple to state but sometimes it can be hard to practice in life, especially when you are "in the thick of it" dealing with circumstances you cannot control. However, the practice of love, reliance, and faith, is where you can experience strength and renewal.

Whether or not one "believes" in God's existence doesn't change the fact that God is sovereign over all. Circumstances and crises sometimes point us, if not "force" us to trust in God, regardless of our stages of growth, belief, practice, and reliance upon Him.

Let me offer an example. Ever since age twelve, I have been a student of the life of Abraham Lincoln, the 16th President of the United States, whose administration lasted from 1861 - 1865. I have read countless books on his life, many more than once, and written five books on Lincoln, myself. (Please see www.glenaubrey.com)

My driving quest for knowledge of this man originally started as an interest in effective leadership that saw him rise from "nothing" (as he was quoted saying in reference to his upbringing, "The short and simple annals of the poor…") to the highest elected office in the land.

During his life, Mr. Lincoln became more than a little acquainted with the God of the Bible, though as a youth he was said to not believe in light of what he witnessed as Biblical faith and practice. Interestingly, nowhere is it recorded accurately and definitively, at least according to my study, that Mr. Lincoln was a person we could call "Christian" as the term is usually used today. There remains debate on that assessment, clearly.

Well, the reason I bring him up is this: in our nation's deepest crises of a Civil War which lasted for his entire presidency and started even before he was first inaugurated (seven states had left the union a month before he took office), and given the immense sacrifice on both sides of the North and South of hundreds of thousands of lives in bloody conflict, Lincoln often turned to God. He sought a higher wisdom than his own. His belief and public expression of belief in God's involvement in the affairs of mankind grew immensely as the war progressed and neared an end. In fact, in his Second Inaugural Address delivered on March 4, 1865, he used many quotations from the Holy Bible.

He knew the Bible well. It is remembered that he regularly kept a Bible on his desk and often quoted from it.

One memorable statement he made about facing the horrendous crisis of war was this one: "I have been driven many times upon my knees by the overwhelming conviction

that I had nowhere else to go. My own wisdom and that of all about me seemed insufficient for that day."
https://www.goodreads.com/quotes/38057

The point? When it appears we "have nowhere else to go" and our human wisdom seems insufficient to help us effectively deal with the crises we face, we can turn to God, and we should. Consider this option: let's turn to Him sooner … whenever any crisis starts to occur or crosses our path.

There is an overriding truth here. It is this: we can trust God first in everything and not lean or rely on our own understanding. In all our ways, we can acknowledge Him, first and foremost. Let us willingly choose to follow this injunction:

> Proverbs 3: 5-6: 5 Trust in the LORD with all your heart and lean not on your own understanding; 6 in all your ways submit to him, and he will make your paths straight.

Our desire to willingly submit to God, trusting Him no matter what crises we face is where strength originates that helps us endure, do right and God-birthed actions as we learn and understand them, and eventually triumph through His grace and power. It is His doing *through* us. When we submit, we win.

Evangelist Billy Graham was quoted as saying: "I've read the last page of the Bible; it's all going to turn out all right." www.goodreads.com› quotes › 148871-i-ve-read-the-last...

Your crisis is your opportunity to trust God more, requesting and living in His strength, wisdom, and love, no matter how costly the effects of the crisis may be. His love wins. It always does.

Epilogue
The Conclusion
Psalm 91 ... Make It Personal

September 1, 2020

When I was quite young, my mother and father used to read and quote Psalm 91. That passage was used often in our home. Back in those days, all we had was the King James Version of the Holy Bible (KJV).

Mom and Dad employed an easy yet deliberate method to help my young mind understand the great truths of the comfort of God. Likely they had borrowed the method from other Christian families.

I want to share that method with you ... I still use it freely with myself and others today. It is quite simple really, yet profound, at least to my thinking. Regardless of the version of the Bible you are using, wherever you see a reference not to God but to the person you are reading to, or quoting for yourself, just substitute your name or the name of the one (or ones) with whom you are sharing this precious scripture. The words described are underlined in the passage.

Here is Psalm 91 (NIV):

1 Whoever dwells in the shelter of the Most High will rest in the shadow of the Almighty.

2 I will say of the LORD, "He is my refuge and my fortress, my God, in whom I trust."

3 Surely he will save you from the fowler's snare and from the deadly pestilence.

4 He will cover you with his feathers, and under his wings you will find refuge; his faithfulness will be your shield and rampart.

5 You will not fear the terror of night, nor the arrow that flies by day,

6 nor the pestilence that stalks in the darkness, nor the plague that destroys at midday.

7 A thousand may fall at your side, ten thousand at your right hand, but it will not come near you.

8 You will only observe with your eyes and see the punishment of the wicked.

9 If you say, "The LORD is my refuge," and you make the Most High your dwelling,

10 no harm will overtake you, no disaster will come near your tent.

11 For he will command his angels concerning you to guard you in all your ways;

12 they will lift you up in their hands, so that you will not strike your foot against a stone.

13 You will tread on the lion and the cobra; you will trample the great lion and the serpent.

14 "Because he loves me," says the LORD, "I will rescue him; I will protect him, for he acknowledges my name.

15 He will call on me, and I will answer him; I will be with him in trouble, I will deliver him and honor him.

16 With long life I will satisfy him and show him my salvation."

*****

The "I found it!" campaign launched by Campus Crusade for Christ in the 70s was a tool of evangelism. It was effective. You are invited to Google the "I found it evangelistic campaign." I remember the campaign well. In San Diego, California, you probably could not travel too many freeway miles without seeing large billboards with those words: "I found it!" followed by "You can find it, too!" I have been impressed with Campus Crusade for Christ (now Cru), ever since I had association with them beginning in the 70s. I have dear friends and former clients who are involved in Cru right now.

Today more than ever, the phrase "I found it" could also be effectively used in reference to God's peace, comfort, assurance, strength, and renewal, especially in times of crisis for those who seek God. We can find God's person and presence just by asking for Him to come near to us and indwell us.

One of our Creative Team Publishing authors is Skip Vaccarello. Skip wrote a book which is described on our publishing website. The title of the book: ***Finding God in Silicon Valley * Spiritual Journeys in a High-Tech World***. I list the book in the Resources section which follows this conclusion because Skip's book could offer positive influences in your life. The stories of finding God are remarkable and true.

God is present. He is not hidden. He is not uninvolved. He is near to you and me *right now*. He wants us to be close to Him more than life's breath itself. He *can* be found by anyone who seeks Him.

As one youth pastor of mine said many years ago, "If you don't feel close to God, guess who moved..."

We should draw closer to God willfully at all times, but especially in the realities of crises like a pandemic of 2020, growing uncertainties regarding finances, the loss of friends or family members to death no matter the cause, in our grief, when we hear upsetting news of any kind, in confronting the detestable events marking racism and more; *yes, through any crisis we face.*

The choice of the title of this book was intentional: ***God's Plan Unfolding * Strength and Renewal in Times of Crisis*** tells us that while God does not cause evil, He permits us to endure evil's presence and pain at times to increase our faith and our willful dependence on God. His Plan *is* unfolding before our eyes. We are part of it. Our responsibility is to pray to receive strength and renewal through a relationship with God. We then must accept His provision by faith, and share His provision with those around us.

I want to encourage you to draw close to God in all ways, as you face crises and challenges, large or small, in your life. God is faithful. He calls us to be faithfully committed to Him.

Will you renew or initiate your relationship with God?

"Now is the accepted time; behold, now is the day of salvation." (2 Corinthians 6:2b)

"Now is the accepted time; behold, now is the day of salvation." (2 Corinthians 6:2b)

Resources

You are invited to consider and secure these encouraging books, written by nationally known authors. These authors are published by various publishers. Collectively their messages of truth are applicable in this day and age, and in any crisis or situation. In short, their contents are "timeless."

These writers have chosen proven stories, rock solid truths, and instructions on faith, resilience, endurance, Bible prophecy, trusting God, and owning personal responsibility to make oneself better, striving to the utmost to be the best one can be while trusting, obeying, and depending on God.

While absolute perfection is not an achievable goal this side of eternity, perseverance birthed in faith and truth certainly is. We are told, "With God all things are possible." (Matthew 19:26) And Paul writes this motivational sentence in Philippians 3:14: "I press on toward the goal to win the prize for which God has called me heavenward in Christ Jesus." A few verses later he says in Philippians 4:13 and 19:
13 "I can do all this through him who gives me strength."
19 "And my God will meet all your needs according to the riches of his glory in Christ Jesus."

Crises, in one form or another, can touch us all. These circumstances can occur without warning. Let us therefore be strong in the Lord, unwavering in faith, confident that God is in charge, and resolved to serve Him no matter what. That is the message in a nutshell of these contributors. Their proclamations are words of love, faith, hope, and endurance.

May you be informed, blessed, and encouraged as you investigate these resources for yourself.

From the writings of the Apostle Paul:

1 Thessalonians 4:18
"Wherefore comfort one another with these words."
King James Version (KJV)

*****

Aubrey, Glen:

1. ***Faith Matters * The Breakthrough You Want*** (2019)
   ISBN 9780997951974
   Website: www.FaithMattersToYou.com
2. ***God's Plan Unfolding * Strength and Renewal in Times of Crisis*** (2020)
   ISBN 9781735018928
   Website: www.GodsPlanUnfolding.com
3. ***My Awesome Humility and How I Attained It*** (2018)
   ISBN 9780997951950
   Website: www.MyAwesomeHumility.com

Burgess, Terry:

When Our Blue Star Turned Gold (2018)
ISBN 9780997951967
Website: www.goldstarparent.com

Chrysler, Mark A.:

Authentic Hope * Experiencing God's Presence Even When You Are an Unwilling Participant (2020)
ISBN 978-0-9855979-4-8
Website: www.CreativeTeamPublishing.com

Dees, Robert F.:

1. ***Resilient Warriors*** (2011)
   ISBN 9780983891949
2. ***Resilient Warriors Advance Study Guide*** (2012)
   ISBN 9780983891956
3. ***Resilient Leaders*** (2013)
   ISBN 9780985597993
4. ***Resilient Nations*** (2014)
   ISBN 9780989797566
5. ***Resilience God Style*** (2018)
   ISBN 9780997951929
6. ***Resilience God Style Study Guide*** (2018)
   ISBN 9780997951936
   Website: www.ResilienceGodStyle.com

Emra, John:

1. ***Cornerstones and Core Needs of Growing Kids*** (2011)
   ISBN 9780983891901
2. ***Parenting from the Top of the Mountain*** (2011)
   ISBN 9780983891918
3. ***Seven Steps to the Top of the Mountain*** (2012)
   ISBN 9780983891925
   Website: www.LifeIsFullOfChoices.org

Evans, Jimmy and Lucado, Max:

Tipping Point: The End is Here (2020)
ISBN 9781950113347
Buy through Amazon:
https://smile.amazon.com/s?k=tipping+point+jimmy+evans&i=stripbooks&crid=2XJC9IXKH534G&sprefix=tippimg%2Caps%2C198&ref=nb_sb_ss_sc_4_7

Garlow, James L.:

Well Versed: Biblical Answers to Today's Tough Issues (2016)
ISBN 9781621575504
Buy through Amazon:
https://smile.amazon.com/Well-Versed-Biblical-Answers-Todays/dp/1621575500/ref=sr_1_2?crid=1HOTMTJ7H274T&dchild=1&keywords=well+versed+by+jim+garlow&qid=1596996490&s=books&sprefix=well%2Caps%2C208&sr=1-2

Hathaway, Will:

1. ***What If God Is Like This?*** (2011)
   ISBN 9780983891932
2. ***The Human Side of Christ*** (2013)
   ISBN 9780988493421
3. ***Naked*** (2016)
   ISBN 9780996794640
   Website: www.will-hathaway.com

Hendrickson, Everett (Bud):

Enjoy Your Journey * Ten Bedrock Truths to Improve Everything About You (2016)
ISBN Softcover 9780996794633
ISBN Hardcover 9780996794626
Website: **www.EnjoyandImprove.com**

Redd, Richard (Rick):

1. ***All-In or Nothing * Master Your Destiny*** (2020)
   ISBN 9781735018904
2. ***All-In or Nothing * A Guide for Advanced Study of Comprehensive Mastery * Achieve Excellence in Sport and Life*** (2020)
   ISBN 9781735018911
   Website: www.all-inornothing.com

Vaccarello, Skip:

1. ***Finding God in Silicon Valley * Spiritual Journeys in a High-Tech World***
   ISBN 9780996371926
2. ***Finding God in Silicon Valley * Spiritual Journeys in a High-Tech World Interactive Study Guide and Workbook***
   ISBN 9780996371933
   Website: www.skipvaccarello.com

Willey, Barry:

1. ***Out of the Valley * An Amazing Life Story That Can Help You Make Good Choices... and Leave an Eternal Legacy*** (2015)
   ISBN Softcover 9780996371957
   ISBN Hardcover 9780996371964
2. ***Extreme Investing * Changing the World One Believer at a Time*** (2015)
   ISBN Softcover 9780996371940
   ISBN Hardcover 9780996371971
   Website: **www.investingthatmatters.com**

Williams, Angela:

Knowing You Have Done Your Best * No Regrets (2019)
ISBN 9780997951981
Website: **www.knowingyouhavedoneyourbest.com**

Wolf, Larry:

1. ***A Black and White Decision * Why George Zimmerman Was Found Innocent * Why America Must Honor the Memory of Travon Martin*** (2013)
   ISBN 9780989797559
2. ***Policing Peace * What America Can Do Now to Avoid Future Tragedies*** (2017)
   ISBN 9780990339830
   Website: www.policingpeace.com

Products

Books published by Creative Team Publishing and
referenced in
***God's Plan Unfolding* ***
Strength and Renewal in Times of Crisis
are listed and described at this website:
www.CreativeTeamPublishing.com

Order any through:
Amazon.com
barnesandnoble.com

The Author

I enjoy traveling, especially to Gettysburg, Washington, D.C., Europe, and the Middle East. I treasure multi-cultural experiences and am fulfilled when conducting conference center presentations and speaking engagements. Enjoyments in life include walking, bicycle riding, and being with family and close friends; also a fireplace, my dogs, listening to classical music and profound artistic works. I appreciate, compose, and arrange multiple styles of music. I earnestly engage in creatively stimulating conversations on uplifting topics, listening and responding to other people's well-thought-out perspectives. I love to laugh. I thoroughly enjoy good football and baseball games. I am a student and teacher, a follower and leader.

Further, "I acknowledge that I have a long way to go in learning what life is all about. I acknowledge that I am willing to work hard to achieve what I believe I am called to do. I also willingly and joyfully acknowledge dependence on God."

~ From *Lincoln – The Making of a Leader* by Glen Aubrey © 2017

The Publisher

Creative Team Publishing (CTP)

If you are an author: "We Want to Publish Your Creation!"

www.CreativeTeamPublishing.com

You are invited to contact Glen Aubrey for
products and services.

www.glenaubrey.com

www.ingramcontent.com/pod-product-compliance
Lightning Source LLC
Chambersburg PA
CBHW031104080526
44587CB00011B/815
9781735018928